Editor

Mara Ellen Guckian

Cover Artist

Brenda DiAntonis

Editor in Chief

Karen J. Goldfluss, M.S. Ed.

Illustrator

Clint McKnight

Imaging

James Edward Grace

Craig Gunnell

Publisher

Mary D. Smith, M.S. Ed.

TCR 3995

DAILY WAR

Language Skills

GRADE 5

Includes Standards and Benchmarks

- Over 150 daily language warm-ups
- Practice in key language skill areas:
  - Parts of Speech
  - Sentence Structure
  - Vocabulary
  - Mechanics and Usage
  - Using Reference Materials
- Each warm-up includes a skill review and a writing activity.

Ideal for Test Preparation!

Author

Mary Rosenberg

Teacher Created Resources, Inc.

6421 Industry Way

Westminster, CA 92683

www.teachercreated.com

ISBN: 978-1-4206-3995-7

© *2009 Teacher Created Resources, Inc.*

Reprinted, 2011

Made in U.S.A.

Teacher Created Resources

TABLE OF CONTENTS

INTRODUCTION

In the *Daily Warm-Ups: Language Skills* series, there are over 150 warm-ups that cover a wide range of writing skills including grammar, mechanics, punctuation, and parts of speech. Each warm-up provides a brief overview of a particular skill, an example of how to use the skill correctly, an activity for the skill, as well as a follow-up writing activity for applying the skill.

The activities in *Daily Warm-Ups: Language Skills* for Grade 5 are ideal for both parents and teachers and are easy to use. To make the most of them, use the Table of Contents (page 2) and Standards Correlation (pages 4–5) to pinpoint specific skills that need to be practiced. The Tracking Sheet (page 6) will assist you and/or the student to keep track of his or her progress.

For parents, select the skill you want to work on with your child and preview the page with him or her. Be sure to have your child note the topic that is being covered. This will allow him or her to access the prior knowledge and information that he or she already knows about the skill. Continue to go over the page with your child so that he or she will know what to do. When your child has completed the page, take a few minutes to correct the work and address any errors made. The answer key starts on page 165.

For the classroom teacher, simply identify the skill page you want to use with the students and photocopy a class set. If several pages are available on a specific skill, you might want to photocopy the pages and make individual packets using the cover on page 7. When presenting a page to your students, start at the top of the page where it notes the topic (skill) that is being covered. By doing this, the students will begin to access the prior knowledge and information they already know about the topic. Then review the first section. This part of the activity page presents information about the topic, as well as how the student will be applying the skill. The "Practice" section has the student independently (or with guidance) apply the skill. The final section—"Write On!"—provides a writing activity that incorporates that page's specific skill.

The skills covered in the *Daily Warm-Ups: Language Skills* series are skills that are used throughout one's life. Helping your child or students master these skills gives them the tools they need to succeed throughout the rest of their educational career and beyond.

STANDARDS CORRELATION

The lessons and activities in this book meet the following standards and benchmarks, which are used with permission from McREL. Copyright 2009 McREL. Mid-continent Research for Education and Learning 4601 DTC Boulevard, Suite 500 Denver, CO 80237 Telephone: 303-337-0990 Website: *www.mcrel.org/standards-benchmarks*

Language Arts Standards

Standard 1: Uses the general skills and strategies of the writing process

- Editing and Publishing: Uses strategies to edit and publish work — 148–160
- Writes expository compositions — 8–14, 19, 23, 29, 32–33, 38–40, 42, 44, 47–38, 50, 54–59, 64, 67, 71, 75, 80, 104, 107, 112, 134, 147, 156, 158
- Writes narrative accounts such as poems and stories — 14, 16–18, 19–24, 35, 61, 68–69, 83, 100, 101, 107
- Writes autobiographical compositions — 14, 16–20, 25, 30, 31, 34–35, 37, 54
- Writes expressive compositions — 11, 14–18, 26–28, 34–37, 44, 49, 50, 53, 56, 62, 78, 99, 110–125, 133
- Writes personal letters — 130
- Writes business letters — 141

Standard 2: Uses the stylistic and rhetorical aspects of writing

- Uses descriptive language — 110–125
- Uses paragraph form in writing — 148–150
- Uses a variety of sentence structures in writing — 55–70

Standard 3: Uses grammatical and mechanical conventions in written compositions

- Uses pronouns in written compositions — 46–54
- Uses nouns in written compositions — 9–15
- Uses verbs in written compositions — 16–24
- Uses adjectives in written compositions — 25–31
- Uses adverbs in written compositions — 32–35
- Uses conjunctions in written compositions — 42–45
- Uses conventions of spelling in written compositions — 71–81, 90–104, 107–109
- Uses conventions of capitalization in written compositions — 126–127, 130, 151–154
- Uses conventions of punctuation in written compositions — 36, 58–70, 126–147, 151–154

Language Arts Standards

Standard 4: Gathers and uses information for research purposes

- Uses dictionaries to gather information — 155–159
- Uses key words, guide words, alphabetical and numerical order, indexes, cross-references, and letters on volumes to find information for research topics — 155–164
- Cites information sources — 160

Standard 5: Uses the general skills and strategies of the reading process

- Uses phonetic and structural analysis techniques, syntactic structure, and semantic context to decode unknown words — 71–82, 90–102
- Uses a variety of context clues to decode unknown words — 90–100
- Uses word reference materials to determine the meaning, pronunciation, and derivations of unknown words — 90–100, 155–159
- Understands level-appropriate reading vocabulary — 71–109

Standard 7: Uses reading skills and strategies to understand and interpret a variety of informational texts

- Knows the defining characteristics of a variety of informational texts   155–164

Teacher Note: Many of the "Write On!" assignments at the bottom of each Warm-Up can be made more specific to meet benchmarks.

TRACKING SHEET

Parts of Speech	Parts of Speech (cont.)	Parts of Speech (cont.)	Sentence Structure	Vocabulary
Page 8	Page 24	Page 41	Page 55	Page 71
Page 9	Page 25	Page 42	Page 56	Page 72
Page 10	Page 26	Page 43	Page 57	Page 73
Page 11	Page 27	Page 44	Page 58	Page 74
Page 12	Page 28	Page 45	Page 59	Page 75
Page 13	Page 29	Page 46	Page 60	Page 76
Page 14	Page 30	Page 47	Page 61	Page 77
Page 15	Page 31	Page 48	Page 62	Page 78
Page 16	Page 32	Page 49	Page 63	Page 79
Page 17	Page 33	Page 50	Page 64	Page 80
Page 18	Page 34	Page 51	Page 65	Page 81
Page 19	Page 35	Page 52	Page 66	Page 82
Page 20	Page 36	Page 53	Page 67	Page 83
Page 21	Page 37	Page 54	Page 68	Page 84
Page 22	Page 38		Page 69	Page 85
Page 23	Page 39		Page 70	Page 86
	Page 40			Page 87

Vocabulary (cont.)	Figures of Speech	Punctuation	Mechanics and Editing	Using Reference Materials
Page 88	Page 110	Page 126	Page 148	Page 155
Page 89	Page 111	Page 127	Page 149	Page 156
Page 90	Page 112	Page 128	Page 150	Page 157
Page 91	Page 113	Page 129	Page 151	Page 158
Page 92	Page 114	Page 130	Page 152	Page 159
Page 93	Page 115	Page 131	Page 153	Page 160
Page 94	Page 116	Page 132	Page 154	Page 161
Page 95	Page 117	Page 133		Page 162
Page 96	Page 118	Page 134		Page 163
Page 97	Page 119	Page 135		Page 164
Page 98	Page 120	Page 136		
Page 99	Page 121	Page 137		
Page 100	Page 122	Page 138		
Page 101	Page 123	Page 139		
Page 102	Page 124	Page 140		
Page 103	Page 125	Page 141		
Page 104		Page 142		
Page 105		Page 143		
Page 106		Page 144		
Page 107		Page 145		
Page 108		Page 146		
Page 109		Page 147		

DAILY WARM-UPS

Name _____   Date _____

Parts of Speech

There are eight parts of speech. The **eight parts of speech** are *nouns*, *verbs*, *adjectives*, *adverbs*, *interjections*, *prepositions*, *conjunctions*, and *pronouns*.

Nouns—name people, places, or things

Verbs—identify actions or states of being

Adjectives—describe nouns or pronouns

Adverbs—describe verbs

Interjections—show strong emotion

Prepositions—relate nouns or pronouns to other words in the sentence

Conjunctions—connect words or groups of words

Pronouns—replace nouns in a sentence

PRACTICE

Identify the part of speech for each underlined word.

Example: We went to the store <u>and</u> we went to the zoo. <u>conjunction</u>

1. The stars <u>twinkled</u> in the night sky. _____

2. "<u>Wait</u>!" yelled the kid. _____

3. <u>It</u> stopped on the line. _____

4. The cars traveled <u>slowly</u> in the rush hour traffic. _____

5. The cement dried <u>quickly</u> in the hot sun. _____

6. Dad baked the cake, <u>and</u> he broiled the chicken. _____

7. My homework is <u>in</u> my backpack. _____

8. The television is <u>on</u> top of the dresser. _____

9. <u>Mr. Neilsen</u> was screaming at the ducks. _____

10. <u>We</u> went to the local school carnival. _____

11. "<u>Ouch</u>!" yelled Marsha. _____

12. The flag <u>waves</u> in the blowing wind. _____

13. Who went to <u>River View Elementary School</u>? _____

14. The <u>wrinkled</u> blanket was thrown over a chair. _____

WRITE ON!

On a separate sheet of paper, write a paragraph on a topic of your choice. Have a classmate underline one example for each part of speech used in the paragraph.

Name _____   Date _____

Common Nouns

A **common noun** names a person, place, or thing. A common noun is not capitalized unless it begins a sentence.

Examples: The boy went to the store to get milk.
boy is a common noun naming a person
store is a common noun naming a place
milk is a common noun naming a thing

Write common nouns for each category. The first one has been done for you.

Person	Place	Thing
1. uncle	1. cafeteria	1. winter
2.	2.	2.
3.	3.	3.
4.	4.	4.
5.	5.	5.
6.	6.	6.
7.	7.	7.
8.	8.	8.

Underline the common nouns in each sentence. The first one has been done for you.

1. My <u>neighbor</u> went to the <u>desert</u> over the <u>summer</u>.
2. The boys like to count the cars that pass by.
3. He was the designer.
4. The family went to eat at the restaurant.
5. The appliances were made by a manufacturer.
6. Did you go to a private school or a public school?
7. The principal drives a red truck.
8. The two brothers practiced riding their skateboards at the old park.
9. Did you follow a special recipe for making pudding pie?
10. That event marked the third volcano to erupt this year.

On a separate sheet of paper, write a paragraph on a topic of your choice. Underline the common nouns used in the paragraph.

Proper Nouns

A **proper noun** is capitalized and names a specific person, place, or thing. Compare the following columns.

	Common Nouns	**Proper Nouns**
Person	boy	Brandon
Place	library	Ronald Reagan Library
Thing	car	Corvette

PRACTICE

Write a proper noun for each common noun.

Example: a friend <u>Suzy</u>

1. an airline _____
2. a teacher _____
3. a state _____
4. a restaurant _____
5. a book _____
6. an artist _____
7. a school _____
8. a toy _____
9. a pet _____
10. a shoe _____

11. a neighbor _____
12. a city _____
13. a country _____
14. a store _____
15. a movie _____
16. a park _____
17. a street _____
18. a game _____
19. a doctor _____
20. a lady _____

Use proper nouns (and your imagination) to complete the story.

Last night, _____ and I went to the movies. The movie, _____ _____, was playing at the _____. The movie starred _____ as the cowboy. The starring actress was _____. The director was _____. The entire movie was filmed on a ranch in _____. The movie has won many prizes and awards, including the _____!

WRITE ON!

On a separate sheet of paper, write a paragraph about a favorite movie. Who starred in the movie? What was the setting for the movie? Underline the proper nouns used in the paragraph.

Name _____   Date _____

Collective Nouns

A noun names a person, place, or thing. A **collective noun** names a group. Groups have members. The members may be people, animals, or things.

Examples:
The *army* has many members.
The *class* of skydivers jumped together.
Our *school* is number one in all academic events!
The *team* is having a great winning streak!

PRACTICE

Underline the collective noun in each sentence.

Example: The <u>armada</u> of ships sailed into the harbor.

1. The army of ants ate the entire tree.

2. You can find it in the atlas of maps.

3. The band plays at every festival and local event.

4. The board of directors is in favor of raising the entrance fees.

5. The troop of baboons threw fruit at the fence.

6. The swarm of flies landed on the windowsill.

7. The school of fish swims together all over the ocean.

8. Did you hear the brood of chicks cheeping in the barn?

9. Moosie had her litter yesterday.

10. The cast of the play went on strike over the quality of the scripts.

11. Mom bought a bunch of bananas at the market.

12. I watched the flock fly south.

13. The mob of kangaroos set up camp in the outback.

14. The pool of word processors is filled with many speedy typists.

15. I took the roll of coins to the bank.

WRITE ON!

On a separate sheet of paper, write a paragraph using at least five collective nouns. Exchange papers with a classmate and underline the collective nouns in each other's paragraphs.

Name _____ Date _____

Collective Nouns

Nouns name people, places and things. A **collective noun** names a group. Groups have members. The members may be people, animals, or things.

When the members of the collective noun are doing the same thing, the collective noun is *singular*.

    Example: The *team* climbs the rope ladders.

When the members of the collective noun are doing different things, the collective noun is *plural*.

    Example: The *team* climb the rope ladders, run up and down the bleachers, and do push ups.

Underline the sentence in each group with the plural collective noun.

1. The armada of ships was from Spain. There were nine ships in the armada. The armada unfurl their sails, raise their anchors, and set sail for new lands.

2. The cast of actors is on strike. The cast have issues with food, working conditions, and pay. The cast will continue to strike until their demands are met.

3. The squad of players went to the championship. The squad hopes to win the tournament. The squad excel in defense, offense, and surprise tactics.

4. The brood of chickens is in the chicken coop. The brood sleep, eat, and lay eggs in their nests. Each day, the farmer goes to the coop to collect the eggs that the brood has laid.

5. The mob of kangaroos is on exhibit at the zoo. The mob enjoy boxing, hopping, and swinging their tails at each other. The mob is a big favorite with the visitors.

6. The bunch of bananas fell from the tree. The bunch had six bananas. The bunch were bruised, broken, and split in half.

Write a paragraph using a collective noun. Exchange papers with a classmate. Have a classmate identify the sentence with the collective noun and decide if it was used in its singular or its plural form.

Name _____ Date _____

Possessive Nouns

A **noun** names a person, place, thing, or idea.

Examples: actor, studio, set, fame

A **proper noun** names a specific person, place, thing, or idea. A proper noun begins with a capital letter.

Examples: Jackie Starlet, Hollywood, *On the Lot* (a movie)

A **possessive noun** shows ownership.

Example: Jackie Starlet's character in *On the Lot* was very believable.

- To make a singular noun possessive, add an apostrophe s ('s) to the end of the noun.
  Example: John's truck
- If the singular noun ends in an *s*, add an apostrophe to the end of the noun. You can also add an apostrophe s ('s) to the end of the noun. Whatever you decide, be consistent.
  Example: Chris' sugar cookies   Example: My boss's bookmark

Write the possessive form of each noun on the line.

Example: taco _taco's_

1. Tess _____
2. fox _____
3. Bob _____
4. Gus _____
5. pencil _____
6. Sis _____
7. watch _____
8. Ross _____
9. pillow _____
10. bank _____

11. anchor _____
12. castle _____
13. beach _____
14. shoe _____
15. bowl _____
16. bus _____
17. song _____
18. boss _____
19. television _____
20. desk _____

Underline the mistake in each sentence. Write the word correctly on the line.

Example: The <u>beaches</u> sand was warm. _beach's_

1. The foxes den was filled with soft grasses and leaves. _____
2. The buckets handle was broken. _____
3. The shoes'es heels broke off. _____
4. Where is Dads' bike? _____

On a separate sheet of paper, describe a favorite item. Rewrite the description making errors in the use of the possessive nouns. Exchange papers with a classmate. Have the classmate underline the mistakes.

Name _____ Date _____

Appositives

An **appositive** renames the noun in the sentence. Appositives are set off by commas or hyphens.

Examples:

Dr. Martens, the optometrist, has his own clinic.

Dr. Martens is the noun.

The *optometrist* is the appositive. It renames the noun.

The cat, Morris, scratched me.

Cat is the noun.

Morris is the appositive. It renames the noun.

Write an appositive for each noun.

Example: Vicki, the landlady, takes good care of the tenants.

1. John, _____, loves to build items out of wood.

2. My parents, _____, like to travel to other countries.

3. Fido, _____, always barks at friends and strangers.

4. My teddy bear, _____, always sleeps on my bed.

5. The red car, _____, ran the red light.

6. The principal, _____, likes it to be absolutely silent in the cafeteria.

7. The new department store, _____, carries a wide selection of clothing and household goods.

8. Did you see the movie, _____?

9. _____, a brand of television, has great picture quality.

10. Have you met my cousin, _____?

Underline the appositives in the paragraph.

   The company, Sewing Brothers Limited, made a whole line of sewing machines. The smallest, Petite Sewer, was made for the beginning sewer. This machine was small in size and easy to use. The second machine, Sew So Easy, was bigger and had more accessories. It could make button holes as well as sew different stitches: zig zag, straight, and whip. The largest machine, The Big Bertha, was a top-of-the-line machine. It had different "feet"—buttons, zippers, and hems—as well as different stitches—plain and fancy. These three machines, The Petite Sewer, Sew So Easy, and The Big Bertha, made life easier for many sewers!

On a separate piece of paper, write about an invention that has made your life easier. Include at least three appositives in the paragraph and underline them.

Name _____   Date _____

Irregular Plural Nouns

Most singular nouns are made plural by adding *-s* or *-es* to the end of the noun.

     Examples: one dog—several dog*s*

                         one dress—many dress*es*

Some nouns do not change form. The noun stays the same for both the singular form and the plural form.

     Example: one sheep—ten sheep

Irregular plural nouns change form when going from singular to plural.

     Examples: one child—three children

                         one leaf—eight leaves

PRACTICE

Write the plural form for each word. The first one has been done for you.

1. deer deer
2. scarf _____
3. woman _____
4. fish _____
5. elf _____
6. tooth _____
7. ox _____
8. moose _____

9. half _____
10. wife _____
11. mouse _____
12. sheep _____
13. knife _____
14. man _____
15. goose _____
16. foot _____

Underline the mistake in each sentence. Write the word correctly on the line. The first one has been done for you.

1. The ten <u>mices</u> ran back into the hole. <u>mice</u>
2. The three mens and the lady went to the symphony. _____
3. Santa's elfs are always busy making toys. _____
4. Both halfs of the soccer game were exciting. _____
5. Are wolfs on the endangered species list? _____
6. There were many peoples at the parade. _____
7. The gooses were flying in formation. _____
8. Be careful with the sharp knifes. _____

WRITE ON!

On a separate sheet of paper, write a paragraph using at least four irregular plural nouns. Exchange papers with a classmate. Have the classmate underline the irregular plural nouns.

Name _____ Date _____

Present Tense Verbs

A **present tense verb** tells about an action or event that is happening now.

Example: I *write* stories.

Rewrite each sentence in the present tense. Underline the present tense verbs.

Example: The burglar decided to rob a house.

The burglar <u>decides</u> to rob a house.

1. The burglar sneaked into the dark house.

   _____

2. He climbed through the broken window.

   _____

3. He triggered the silent alarm.

   _____

4. The burglar tip-toed from room to room.

   _____

5. He placed the valuables into his pillowcase.

   _____

6. He climbed down the ladder and his pants caught on a tree branch.

   _____

7. He wriggled in vain to get free.

   _____

8. The burglar dropped the pillowcase to the ground.

   _____

9. The police cars pulled up to the house.

   _____

10. The police officers pointed their flashlights at the squirming burglar.

   _____

Write a paragraph on a separate sheet of paper. Use present tense verbs to tell about what you are doing right now. Have a classmate underline the present tense verbs used in your paragraph.

Name _____   Date _____

Action Verbs

An **action verb** describes an action.

Examples: I *run*. He *reads*. They *kick*.

PRACTICE

Circle the action verbs.

Example: (sleep)

1. think
2. smell
3. touch
4. help
5. up
6. bridge
7. taste
8. down
9. loud
10. laugh

11. play
12. hug
13. hard
14. scream
15. see
16. dresser
17. cry
18. cup
19. feel
20. friend

Underline the action verb in each sentence.

Example: I <u>live</u> in a two-story house.

1. He jumps around like a kangaroo!
2. The camera takes great pictures.
3. Great-Aunt Sally makes the best bread!
4. The car cruises slowly down the street.
5. The rose bushes drink up the sunlight.
6. Professor Fox teaches a class on anthropology.
7. The decorator chooses the paint colors and house furnishings.
8. The alarm company calls when a house alarm is triggered.
9. Taylor Morgan works for an electric company.
10. The coordinates tell where something is located.

WRITE ON!

Write about a favorite activity on a separate sheet of paper. Use action verbs in the paragraph. Underline the action verbs you used.

Name _____ Date _____

Past Tense Verbs

A **past tense verb** tells about an action that has already happened. To make most verbs past tense, add -*ed* to the end of the verbs.

    Examples: finish—finish*ed*   jump—jump*ed*

If the verb ends in a single vowel followed by a single consonant (except *w* or *y*), double the last consonant and add -*ed*.

    Examples: step—step*ped*   mop—mop*ped*

If the verb ends in an *e*, simply add a -*d* to the ending.

    Examples: dance—danc*ed*   glide—glid*ed*

PRACTICE

Write the past tense form for each verb.

    Example: rest <u>rested</u>

1. wrap _____
2. watch _____
3. bake _____
4. cook _____
5. wash _____
6. kick _____

7. clean _____
8. hunt _____
9. stop _____
10. stay _____
11. stab _____
12. nap _____

Rewrite the paragraph in the past tense.

    I watch tonight's football game. Our team plays the best game ever. My brother scores three touchdowns. My cousin tackles two players and punts the ball four times. My family and I cheer and scream until we lose our voices. It is a great game!

_____

_____

_____

_____

_____

WRITE ON!

On a separate sheet of paper, write a paragraph about something that happened to you last week. Underline the past tense verbs used in the paragraph.

Name _____ Date _____

Irregular Verbs

Most verbs are made past tense by adding *–ed* to the end of the verb.

  Examples: finish—finish*ed*   hope—hop*ed*

Some verbs are irregular. Some **irregular verbs** change form and some stay the same.

  Examples: buy—bought
          do—done
          cut—cut
          bet—bet

PRACTICE

Write the past tense form of the verb.

  Example: tell — <u>told</u>

1. catch _____
2. teach _____
3. drink _____
4. build _____
5. freeze _____
6. sting _____
7. hide _____
8. wet _____
9. write _____
10. sing _____

11. keep _____
12. eat _____
13. set _____
14. think _____
15. sell _____
16. slide _____
17. speak _____
18. shut _____
19. say _____
20. sit _____

Underline the mistakes in the paragraph. Write the correct forms of the verbs on the lines below.

    Yesterday, I go to the store. I buyed some fruit, vegetables, bread, milk, and juice. I gived the cashier the money to pay for the groceries. I drived home. When I got home, I putted all the groceries away. Some goed in the cupboard and some went in the refrigerator.

1. _____
2. _____
3. _____

4. _____
5. _____
6. _____

WRITE ON!

On a separate piece of paper, tell about something that happened in the past. It could be about a bad haircut, a test, or the first day of school. Underline the irregular past tense verbs used in the paragraph.

Name _____ Date _____

Linking Verbs

A **linking verb** connects the subject to its complement (information about the subject). By itself, a linking verb does not have much meaning. Most linking verbs are forms of the verb *to be*.

Example: He *is* a student.

Present Tense	Past Tense	Present Tense	Past Tense
I am	I was	We are	We were
You are	You were	You (all) are	You (all) were
He is	He was	They are	They were
She is	She was		
It is	It was		

Choose a linking verb to complete each sentence.

Example: I _____ happy.

I <u>am</u> happy.

1. The boy _____ pleased with the turnout.

2. Dad _____ unsure about how to solve the problem.

3. We _____ excited about the news.

4. Who _____ their president?

5. _____ you sad today?

6. He _____ a soccer player.

7. The TV anchors _____ women.

8. Jack _____ in first place.

9. It _____ a scary movie.

10. The zombie _____ big and slimy.

Write a paragraph on a separate sheet of paper. Tell about a time you lost something important. What did you do to find it? Underline the linking verbs used in your paragraph.

Name _____ Date _____

Future Tense Verbs

The **future tense** is used for newly-made decisions, for giving orders, or to show what will happen in the future.

The future tense is shown by using the word *will* + verb.

Examples:

I will + verb	*I will* read.	*It will* + verb	*It will* read.
You will + verb	*You will* read.	*We will* + verb	*We will* read.
He will + verb	*He will* read.	*They will* + verb	*They will* read.
She will + verb	*She will* read.		

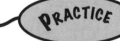

Rewrite each sentence in the future tense.

> Example: I bake a cake.—<u>I will bake a cake.</u>

1. The clock chimes on the hour, every hour.

   _____

2. The bathtub holds about 100 gallons of water.

   _____

3. The couch rolls on casters.

   _____

4. The sun rises in the east.

   _____

5. The golfers tee off every morning at 6:00 A.M. sharp.

   _____

Rewrite the paragraph using the future tense.

   Nina prepared the journalists for the president's speech. The journalists took notes and then sat down on the folding chairs. Soon President Juarez came out and stood behind the podium. She gave a short speech and then answered questions.

_____
_____
_____
_____

What are you planning to do next week? On a separate sheet of paper, write a paragraph about your plans. Use future tense verbs to tell about your plans.

Name _____ Date _____

Future Progressive Tense Verbs

The **future progressive tense** tells about one event going on when something else happens in the future. The future progressive tense is made by using the verb *will be* + *verb* with an *-ing* ending.

Examples:

I *will be going* to class when the bell rings.

You *will be going* to the zoo tomorrow.

He *will be going* home later.

She *will be going* to class with her brother.

It *will be going* on all evening.

We *will be going* hiking next week.

You *will be going* to camp this year.

They *will be going* to class after recess.

Underline the sentences where the future progressive tense is used.

Example: Tony <u>will be answering</u> the phone if no one else shows up.

1. Ryan will be eating all of the doughnuts because no one came to the social.
2. Mr. and Mrs. Sandoval will be painting Marilyn's room while she is camping.
3. Tom and Mark will be making many enchiladas and tamales.
4. Where is Mr. Morrison?
5. Kim will be presenting a report at the next student council meeting.
6. The ocean will be reaching high tide sometime this evening.
7. Have you seen Mrs. O'Connor lately?
8. The striped wallpaper looked beautiful in the living room.
9. The silver mirror was made by a master craftsperson.
10. The telephone will be ringing off the hook as soon as the number is posted.

Write a sentence using the future progressive tense.

_____

_____

Write about an upcoming event (a sleepover, a trip, a game, the weekend) on a separate sheet of paper. Use at least one sentence in the future progressive tense. Underline the future progressive verb.

Name _____ Date _____

Future Perfect Tense Verbs

The **future perfect tense** is used to show something that has not yet been done but that will be done before a set time in the future.

The future perfect tense is made using *will have* + *past tense* verb.

Example: By the time Jeremy arrives, *I will have completed* many math problems.

Underline each sentence where the future perfect tense is used. Rewrite the sentences that are not underlined in the future perfect tense.

Example: <u>By the time Modesto arrives, I will have been running on the treadmill for an hour.</u>

1. Penny will have spent all of her money before the day is over.

   _____

2. The helicopter will have flown for six hours before it lands in Los Angeles.

   _____

3. As of next week, Elise and Jean will have been best friends for twenty years.

   _____

4. The agents have searched the rooms looking for the missing money.

   _____

5. Andre will have spent 20 hours on the plane by the time it lands in Japan.

   _____

6. The frozen drink will have defrosted by the time Mario gets home from school.

   _____

7. Will you see Zoe before the show ends?

   _____

8. I have been to ten Moonlight Socials since January.

   _____

9. Wilhelmina will have changed clothes ten times before she decides on the "perfect" outfit.

   _____

10. By the time Allen arrives at the station, Edith will have waited two hours.

    _____

Have you ever waited a long time for someone to arrive or something to happen? What were you doing while you waited? On a separate sheet of paper, write about the experience using the future perfect tense.

Name _____ Date _____

Future Perfect Progressive Tense Verbs

The **future perfect progressive tense** describes a future, ongoing action that will happen before some specific time in the future.

The future perfect progressive tense is made by using *will have been* + a verb with an *-ing* ending.

Example: I <u>will have been waiting</u> forever before they announce the results of the election!

Underline each sentence where a verb in the future perfect progressive tense is used.

Example: <u>As of next week, Ira will have been flying for one year.</u>

1. I will have been playing chess for 10 years by the time I am 20 years old.

2. Bess will have been painting for 10 hours by the time she stops for dinner.

3. The ship will have been sailing the seas for three years before it docks again.

4. Wilbur will have eaten all of the lasagna.

5. By the end of the New Year's Eve celebration, the band will have been playing for 24 hours.

6. She hung up the phone.

7. Yolanda will have been working on the quilt every day for six months in order to finish it on time for Mother's Day.

8. Has Ian been doing his homework lately?

9. The antique lamp gives off a soft, glowing light when turned on.

10. The taxi will have been waiting at the curb for many hours by the time the plane arrived.

Write two sentences using the future perfect progressive tense.

1. _____

_____

2. _____

_____

On a separate sheet of paper, write about a topic of your choice. Use at least one sentence in the future perfect progressive tense. Underline that sentence.

Name _____   Date _____

Comparative Adjectives

An **adjective** describes a noun.

>   Example: The *old* blanket has many holes in it.

>   *Old* is an adjective. *Old* describes the noun *blanket*.

A **comparative adjective** compares two things.

>   Example: The blanket is *older* than the bedspread.

When forming a comparative adjective, add *-er* to the end of the adjective.

>   Example: Bill is fast. Joanne is *faster* than Bill.

If the adjective ends in *y*, drop the *y* and add *-ier*.

>   Example: I am happy.   I am *happier* than Susie.

> If the adjective has three or more syllables, use the word *more* before the adjective. Do not add *-er* to the end of the adjective.
>
>   Example: William's behavior is outrageous. William's behavior today is *more outrageous* than it was yesterday.

PRACTICE

Write the comparative form for each adjective.

>   Example: stinky   <u>stinkier</u>

1. superficial _____
2. hungry _____
3. thirsty _____
4. natural _____
5. embarrassed _____

6. dirty _____
7. magical _____
8. grumpy _____
9. virtuous _____
10. steep _____

Underline the misspelled comparative adjectives in the paragraph below. Spell the underlined comparative adjectives correctly on the lines below the paragraph.

>   My sister and I are identical twins. We look the same but we do have differences. I am tallyer than Tina. Tina is slightly heavyer than I am. I wear a largeer shoe size than Tina. Tina wears a biger dress size than I do. My eyes are bluyer than Tina's. Her hair is longerer than my hair. Despite these differences, people still cannot tell us apart!

1. _____
2. _____
3. _____

4. _____
5. _____
6. _____

WRITE ON!

On a separate sheet of paper, write a paragraph comparing yourself to one of your siblings or a friend. How are you alike? How are you different? Underline the comparative adjectives used in the paragraph.

Name _____ Date _____

Comparative Adjectives

A **comparative adjective** compares two persons, places, or things.

     Example: The glass is *dirtier* than the dish.

When forming a comparative adjective, add *–er* to the end of the adjective.

     Example: Dad is tall. Grandpa is *taller* than Dad.

If the adjective ends in *y*, drop the *y* and add *ier*.

     Example: The hedgehog is spiky. The porcupine is *spikier* than the hedgehog.

If the adjective has three or more syllables, use the word *more* before the adjective. Do not add *–er* to the end of the adjective.

     Example: Mom is protective of the children.

      The grandmother is *more protective* of the children than the mother is.

PRACTICE

Write the correct form of the comparative adjective on the line.

     Example: (friendly) John is <u>friendlier</u> than Matt.

1. (ugly) Possums are _____ than beavers.
2. (bald) My dad is _____ than Uncle Fred.
3. (rough) Burlap is _____ than silk.
4. (white) You are _____ than a ghost!
5. (healthy) Jeb's diet is _____ than Lincoln's.
6. (choosy) Amber is _____ than Abigail.
7. (short) Jeff is _____ than Cliff.
8. (wild) The monkey is _____ than the ape.
9. (ferocious) The jackal is _____ than the hyena.
10. (chunky) The brand of peanut butter is _____ than the other brand.
11. (pretty) The baby is _____ than her picture.
12. (clear) The lake water is _____ than the city water.
13. (quiet) What animal is _____ than a mouse?
14. (brave) Who is _____ than a soldier?
15. (unbelievable) These stories are _____ than the last ones.

WRITE ON!

Write four comparative sentences on the back of this page. In each sentence make a mistake using the comparative adjective. Exchange papers with a classmate. Have a classmate underline the mistakes and write the comparative adjectives correctly.

Name _____   Date _____

Superlative Adjectives

A **superlative adjective** compares more than two items.

>Example: Sarah is the *quietest* of the three children in the family.

To make a superlative adjective, add *-est* to the end of the adjective.

>Example: A squirrel is small. A guinea pig is smaller. A hedgehog is the *smallest* of the three animals.

If the adjective ends in *y*, drop the *y* and add *-iest* to the end of the adjective.

>Example: This is the *tastiest* pie I have ever eaten!

Do not add *-est* to the end of adjectives with three or more syllables. If the adjective has three or more syllables, use the word *most* before the adjective.

>Example: Mom is the *most organized* person I know.

PRACTICE

Write the correct form of the superlative adjective on the line.

>Example: (sharp) Which animal has the <u>sharpest</u> teeth?

1. (rich) Who is the _____ person in the world?

2. (poisonous) Which snake is the _____?

3. (powerful) Ronald Smyth is the _____ lawyer in town.

4. (outrageous) Bernadette always wears the _____ outfits!

5. (silly) That clown is the _____ one of all.

6. (prestigious) Campbell College is one of the _____ colleges in the nation.

7. (glamorous) Was Ginger Rogers the _____ actress of her time?

8. (pretty) Liz Bird is the _____ model of the year.

9. (ramshackle) That house is the _____ one on the street.

10. (repellant) A skunk has the _____ odor of any animal.

11. (rough) Sandpaper is the _____ material to the touch.

12. (sick) Ralph is the _____ child in the hospital.

13. (flattering) *Sky to the Touch* received the _____ publicity of all the newly published books.

14. (safe) It is the _____ place to store one's valuables.

WRITE ON!

On a separate sheet of paper, write a paragraph on a topic of your choice. Use at least three superlative adjectives. Underline the superlative adjectives used in the paragraph.

DAILY
Warm-Up 21

Irregular Comparative and Superlative Adjectives

Some **comparative** and **superlative adjectives** change form.

Example: This book is *good*.

This book is *better* than the first one.

This book is the *best* one of all.

PRACTICE

Complete the chart showing the different forms for each adjective. If you are not sure of the adjective, use a dictionary to look up the word. The dictionary will show the comparative and superlative forms for the word.

Adjective	Comparative	Superlative
good		
	worse	
		least
much, many, some		
	farther	

Write sentences for each set of irregular comparative and superlative adjectives.

1. (bad, worse, worst)

_____

_____

_____

2. (little, less, least)

_____

_____

_____

3. (many, more, most)

_____

_____

_____

WRITE ON!

On a separate sheet of paper, describe the best gift you were ever given. Use superlative and comparative adjectives to describe the gift and what made it so special.

Name _____   Date _____

Numerical Adjectives

When a number describes a noun, it is called a numerical adjective. A **numerical adjective** is an adjective that tells *how many*.

Example: Rebecca ate *six* cupcakes.

Underline the numerical adjective in each sentence. Write the number represented on the line following the sentence.

Example: Guy has <u>four</u> pairs of shoes. __4__

1. Mark made a dozen cookies. _____

2. Do you have two pencils? _____

3. Where are my thirty action figures? _____

4. I have eight fingers. _____

5. She lost one tooth. _____

6. There are eight theme parks in this state. _____

7. Nine million people live in this city. _____

8. Where are the three pigs? _____

9. One million penguins can live in the rookery. _____

10. Megan picked thirteen apples. _____

11. The celebrity signed two hundred autographs. _____

12. The fitness center is open twenty-four hours a day. _____

13. I wear a size seven ring. _____

14. Sixty-four people came to the wedding. _____

15. There are twelve board members. _____

16. Brandon had lost fifteen pounds at his last weigh-in. _____

Underline the numerical adjectives in the paragraph.

For my twelfth birthday, I had a fabulous outdoor party. Eleven friends came to my party. Instead of presents, each friend brought one or two bags of food to donate to the local food bank. My mom made a chocolate cake with three layers. The cake had two candles on it. One candle was the number one. The other candle was a star. After we ate cake, a dozen of us jumped into the swimming pool. What a great birthday!

On a separate sheet of paper, describe the outfit you are wearing. Be sure to include the number of buttons, pockets, zippers, stripes, etc. that are on the outfit. Underline the numerical adjectives used in the paragraph.

Name _____ Date _____

Indefinite Adjectives

An **indefinite adjective** does not name a specific amount. Some common indefinite adjectives are *any, many, much, few, several, all, some, every,* and *each.*

    Example: Do you have *any* coins?

Underline the indefinite adjective in each sentence.

    Example: <u>Several</u> friends and I went to the swap meet.

1. Many people are vegetarians.

2. There is not much money in my piggy bank.

3. May I have some gum?

4. A lot of people travel.

5. There is plenty of food in the fridge.

6. Did Mrs. Nagel bake enough cookies for the class?

7. I shelved all of the books.

8. My pants have a few holes in them.

9. Did you read any of the book last night?

10. The new student has made many friends.

11. Have you met each candidate?

12. Dad likes all kinds of foods.

13. Joey put each and every toy neatly away.

14. Maurice has some homework tonight.

Underline the indefinite adjectives used in the paragraph.

    Trent had a lot of money in his piggy bank. Trent counted out several dollars and put the money in his pocket. Trent hopped on his bike and went to the comic book store. He spent a few dollars on the latest edition of *Super Hero*. Trent spent more money on candy and gum. When his money was gone, he rode his bike back home.

On a separate sheet of paper, write a paragraph about items you have recently purchased or wanted to purchase. Underline the indefinite adjectives used in the paragraph.

Name _____   Date _____

Predicate Adjectives

A **predicate adjective** follows a linking verb and describes the noun (subject). There are two kinds of linking verbs: forms of the verb *to be,* and intransitive verbs such as *seen*, *smell*, *appear*, *feel*, and *look*.

> Example: He is hungry and tired.
>
> *He* is the subject.
>
> *Hungry and tired* is the predicate adjective phrase. It describes the subject.

Underline the predicate adjective (or predicate adjective phrase) in each sentence.

> Example: Mr. Black is <u>tall</u>.

1. The day was warm and sunny.
2. Mr. Dillon looks fabulous.
3. Ms. Lavender was scared.
4. Amanda is a hard worker.
5. Neil and Vinny are brothers.
6. Jillian is a tough competitor.
7. Jason is the fastest typist.
8. The apple tastes delicious.
9. The skunk's scent smells terrible.
10. Goldilocks was a naughty girl.
11. I have been very sick lately.
12. She will be a great leader.

Write two sentences with a predicate adjective in each.

1. _____

   _____

2. _____

   _____

On a separate sheet of paper, write a paragraph telling about a time you were hurt—riding a skateboard, scraping a knee, falling off the monkey bars, or some other incident. Underline the predicate adjectives used in the paragraph.

Name _____ Date _____

Adverbs

An **adverb** describes a verb, an adjective, or another adverb. An adverb tells *how, when, where, what,* or *how often* something is done.

Examples: Fred arrived *first*. (when)

Avery screamed *loudly*. (how)

The table fits *here*. (where)

Underline the adverb in each sentence. The first one has been done for you.

1. Sabrina and Madeline arrived <u>late</u>.
2. She went to bed early.
3. The Olsens live here.
4. It is very quiet.
5. Stacy leaves early for school.
6. We went shopping yesterday.
7. Buttons ate last.
8. The mouse scurried quickly across the floor.
9. Caitlin skis often.
10. The monster lumbered slowly up the hill.
11. The table goes there.
12. The tree creaked eerily in the wind.
13. The cart rolled soundlessly across the floor.
14. Jason called twice about the puppy.
15. Rick talks endlessly.
16. The author writes new stories daily.
17. Ms. O'Brian jogs nightly.
18. The helicopter landed roughly on the tarmac.
19. The dam overflows regularly in June.
20. The alarm buzzed ominously.

On a separate sheet of paper, write about a current event. Underline the adverbs used in the paragraph.

Name _____ Date _____

Comparative Adverbs

A **comparative adverb** compares two items. To make a comparative adverb, add *-er* to the end of the adverb. If the adverb ends in *-y*, drop the *-y* and add *-ier*.

Example: Dennis jumps high. Sadie jumps *higher* than Dennis.

If the adverb ends in *-ly* or has three or more syllables, use the word *more* before the adverb. Do not add *-er* to the end of the adverb.

Example: Seth writes sloppily. Betsy writes *more* sloppily than Seth.

Underline the adverb in the sentence. Write a new sentence using a comparative adverb. Underline the comparative adverb in the new sentence.

Example: Henry feels happy. Patrick feels <u>happier</u> than Henry.

1. Lily ran fast.

   _____

2. Anna hit the ball hard.

   _____

3. The snail moved slowly.

   _____

4. The whiskers felt rough.

   _____

5. Grandpa snored loudly.

   _____

6. Momma sang softly to the baby.

   _____

7. The dancers leaped gracefully across the stage.

   _____

8. The honey tasted sweet.

   _____

9. The present was wrapped beautifully in foil paper.

   _____

   _____

10. Megan played quietly upstairs in her room.

   _____

On a separate sheet of paper, write a paragraph about how people or animals move. Underline the comparative adverbs used in the paragraph.

Name _____   Date _____

Superlative Adverbs

An adverb describes a verb. An adverb tells how, when, where, what, or how often something is done.

Examples: Gia runs *awkwardly*.   Tom eats *slowly*.   The train is running *late*.

A **superlative adverb** compares three or more items.

To make a superlative adverb, add -*est* to the end of the adverb. If the adverb ends in -*y*, drop the -*y* and add -*iest*.

Examples: Michelle's breath smells *yucky*. (adverb)
Ricky's project smells *yuckier* than Michelle's. (comparative adverb)
Brady's project smells the *yuckiest* of all. (superlative adverb)

If the adverb ends in -*ly* or has three or more syllables, do not add -*est* to the end of the word. Instead, use the word *most* before the adverb.

Examples: Zack cuts *carefully* on the lines. (adverb)
Ralph cuts *more carefully* on the lines than Zack. (comparative adverb)
Raiza cuts the *most carefully* of all. (superlative adverb)

PRACTICE

Write a new sentence using a superlative adverb.

1. The baby chortled more happily in his crib than his friend in the playpen.

   _____

2. The surgeon scrubbed more carefully than the nurse.

   _____

3. The dress was knit more delicately than the sweater.

   _____

4. The gown was sewn more carefully than the jacket.

   _____

5. The cat mewed more pitifully than the kitten.

   _____

6. The driver drove slower down the street than the cabbie.

   _____

7. The green grass grew quicker than the weeds in the summer heat.

   _____

WRITE ON!

On a separate sheet of paper, write a paragraph telling about a time you completed a difficult task. How did you feel when you were done? Underline the superlative adverbs used in the paragraph.

Irregular Comparative and Superlative Adverbs

Some adverbs change form when used in the comparative or superlative form.

Adverb	Comparative Adverb	Superlative Adverb
well	better	best
badly	worse	worst
much	more	most
little	less	least
near	nearer	nearest or next
far	farther or further	farthest or furthest
late	later	latest or last

Write a sentence for the type of adverb suggested in parentheses at the beginning of the line.

Example: I feel *sick*.

(superlative) I feel *sickest* of all the people in my family.

1. Margo lives the nearest to Grandma.

    (adverb) _____

2. Kenneth arrived late to the award ceremony.

    (comparative adverb) _____

3. Ms. Eames drove farther than Mr. Giles to attend the meeting.

    (superlative adverb) _____

4. Who lives nearer to the park?

    (adverb) _____

5. Liam lost the most weight.

    (comparative adverb) _____

6. I have more money than my sister.

    (adverb) _____

7. Janine arrived last.

    (comparative adverb) _____

8. Sam did better on the test than Tony.

    (superlative adverb) _____

WRITE ON!

On a separate sheet of paper, write about a time you were sick. Underline the irregular, comparative, or superlative adverbs used in the paragraph.

Name _____ Date _____

Interjections

An **interjection** is a word or a group of words that show feeling.

Use a *comma* after a mild interjection.

> Example: *Well*, the test will be over soon.

Use an *exclamation point* after a strong interjection.

> Example: *Wow!* Did you see the frog catch the fly?

PRACTICE

Write or complete a sentence to accompany each interjection.

> Example: Stop! A train is coming!

1. Whoa, _____

   _____

2. Stop! _____

   _____

3. Ouch! _____

   _____

4. Wow! _____

   _____

5. Oh, no! _____

   _____

6. Hurry up! _____

   _____

7. Oh well, _____

   _____

8. Nonsense, _____

   _____

9. Shh, _____

   _____

10. Aha, _____

    _____

WRITE ON!

On a separate sheet of paper, write about a time you were stung by a bee or hit by a ball. (If this did not really happen, use your imagination.) What did you say? How did you feel? Underline the interjections used in the paragraph.

Name _____   Date _____

Interjections

An **interjection** is a word or a group of words that show feeling. Punctuation after an interjection is determined by the level of emotion.
Use a *comma* after a mild interjection.
    Example: *Yes*, I can help you.
Use an *exclamation point* after a strong interjection.
    Example: *What*! I can't hear you!

PRACTICE

Underline the interjections in each paragraph.

1. You are not going to believe this! I made a complete replica of my house out of toothpicks. You heard right, toothpicks. I entered the replica in a contest. Get this! I won! Can you believe it? I won the contest. First place is one million boxes of toothpicks. Oh, no! What am I going to do with all of those toothpicks? Would you like to build a replica of your house?

2. Well, I was walking to school when suddenly a well-dressed wolf was in front of me. Yes, you heard correctly. It was a real wolf. He reached in my backpack and ate my homework. What? You don't believe me! Oh well, I didn't think you would.

3. That's a beautiful necklace. I can't believe you made it! Awesome! I love all of the beads you used. It must have taken you a long time to make it. Can you make one for me, too? Hurray!

4. Cheryl entered her turnip in the State Fair. Wow! The turnip was huge! Cheryl was hoping it would win first place for being the biggest turnip. Yippee! Cheryl won first place.

5. Congratulations! You are the winner of the Writer's Digest Sweepstake Contest. The first place prize is one million dollars. To claim your prize simply call our headquarters in Maine. If you do not have a phone, you can send us a letter or an e-mail. Well, that's all for now. We look forward to hearing from you soon.

6. Touchdown! Our team scored a touchdown! Now we will get to compete for the pig skin against East Ridge High School. Our school, North Ridge High School, hasn't won the pig skin game in 20 years. Hurray! Now is our chance to redeem ourselves!

WRITE ON!

On a separate sheet of paper, write about an exciting event or time in your life. Underline the interjections used in the paragraph.

Name _____ / _____   Date _____

Prepositional Phrases

A **preposition** is a word or group of words preceding a noun or pronoun. Prepositions show a relationship between an object and another word in the sentence. Common prepositions include the following: *about, above, across, after, at, below, beneath, but, by, beside, during, except, for, in addition to, in spite of, into, on, over, under, until,* and *with.*

A **prepositional phrase** is a group of words made up of a preposition, the object of the preposition, and all of the words in between. A preposition never stands alone. It *always* has an object.

Examples:

Abby put the book on the table. *On the table* is the prepositional phrase.

on is the preposition

table is the object of the preposition

the is the word in between the preposition and the object of the preposition

I got in the car with my new puppy. *With my new puppy* is the prepositional phrase.

with is the preposition

puppy is the object of the preposition

my new are the words in between the preposition and the object of the preposition

PRACTICE

Underline the prepositional phrase or phrases in each sentence.

Example: The baby is sleeping <u>in the crib.</u>

1. Jason ate with his hands, in spite of the rule.
2. Bob and Cherry climbed to the very top of the tree.
3. Mohammed fixed all of the computers in the building.
4. Carole is a top-notch athlete in addition to being a good sport.
5. He rode the sled to the bottom.
6. The car was stored in the parking garage.
7. Gary and his wife travel all around the world.
8. Fresno, in the heart of the Central Valley, is known for its agricultural economy.
9. Ricky gave the receipts to Paula.
10. Cyrus has played many parts, both big and small, in many hit movies.

WRITE ON!

On a separate sheet of paper, write about the perfect car. What would the car look like? What kinds of things could the car do? Underline the prepositional phrases used in the paragraph. Try to have at least three different prepositional phrases in your paragraph.

Name _____ Date _____

Prepositional Phrases

A **prepositional phrase** is a group of words made up of a preposition, the object of the preposition, and all of the words in between. Some prepositional phrases describe a spatial relationship, telling where something is located.

Example: The picture is above the bed. *Above the bed* is a prepositional phrase telling where the picture is located.

above is the preposition

bed is the object of the preposition

the is the word in between the preposition and the object of the preposition

Write a sentence with a prepositional phrase for each prepositional word.

Example: (beside) Put the book beside the magazines.

1. (against) _____

_____

2. (around) _____

_____

3. (within) _____

_____

4. (in front of)_____

_____

5. (near) _____

_____

6. (behind) _____

_____

7. (through) _____

_____

8. (out of) _____

_____

On a separate sheet of paper, describe the placement of items in and on your desk. Underline the prepositional phrases used in each sentence.

Name _____ Date _____

Prepositional Phrases

A **prepositional phrase** is a group of words made up of a preposition, the object of the preposition, and all of the words in between. There can be more than one prepositional phrase in a sentence.

    Example: The jacket was hung beside the front door.

      beside is the preposition.

      door is the object of the preposition.

      the front are the words in between the preposition and the object of the preposition.

Some prepositional phrases describe time.

    Example: Since our move, we have been very busy unpacking.

    Since our move is the prepositional phrase telling about a certain time.

PRACTICE

Underline the prepositional phrase in each sentence. If the phrase describes a time, write a **T** on the line.

    Example: <u>T</u>   <u>By now</u>, the plane should have landed.

1. _____ On Sunday, Mom spends the day baking bread.

2. _____ We all started gathering around lunchtime.

3. _____ Return the postage-paid envelope within ten days.

4. _____ The package was placed beside the front door.

5. _____ During a snowstorm, it is best to stay inside where it is warm and safe.

6. _____ Until dinner time, you need to study for the test.

7. _____ I walked to the other side.

8. _____ All the mail was delivered by 2:00 P.M.

9. _____ For some students, spelling is a difficult skill.

10. _____ The teacher will give us a pre-test on Tuesday morning.

11. _____ Angelo, the weather man, delivers the weather news at 10:00 A.M.

12. _____ There is a roadblock by the river.

13. _____ I had to take my little brother to the mall.

14. _____ Inside the squirrel's home, there are many nuts stored.

15. _____ The travelers unpacked their bags at the hotel.

WRITE ON!

On a separate sheet of paper, write about an appointment, a meeting, or an event. Underline the prepositional phrases that describe a time.

Name _____   Date _____

Prepositional Phrases

A **prepositional phrase** is a group of words made up of a preposition, the object of the preposition, and all of the words in between.

Some **prepositional phrases** describe direction.

    Examples:

      She jumped into the swimming pool.

      into the swimming pool is the prepositional phrase describing the direction (where) she jumped.

      The plane landed on the tarmac.

      on the tarmac is the prepositional phrase describing the direction (where) the plane landed.

PRACTICE

Circle *only* the prepositional phrases that tell about *direction*. Underline the prepositions in those phrases.

    Example: Put the paper into the folder.

1. During an electrical storm, be careful not to touch anything made of metal.

2. I will go to the grocery store.

3. Did you look beneath the couch?

4. Over the hill is a small fruit stand.

5. Let's go onto the escalator.

6. Put the extra house key under the potted plant.

7. Except for a couple of students, everyone else returned their homework.

8. They went into the haunted house.

9. We received a package from Grandma.

10. The pots and pans go below the stove.

11. The class climbed onto the train.

12. The backyard is through this door.

13. The dog tagged along when we went for our walk.

14. The new neighbors went into the restricted area.

15. We walked toward the historical monument.

WRITE ON!

On the back of this page, write a paragraph about somewhere you went last week. Underline the prepositional phrases that refer to a specific direction. Use at least two.

Name _____ Date _____

DAILY
Warm-Up 35

Conjunctions

A **conjunction** joins words to words, phrases to phrases, and sentences to sentences. The parts joined by the sentence must be "equal" or parallel. Equal or parallel phrasing uses verbs of the same tense.

Example of parallel phrasing: I like to *wash* my car and *clean* the wheels.

Example of non-parallel phrasing: I enjoyed *washing* my car and *cleaned* the wheels.

PRACTICE

Rewrite each sentence so that the phrasing is equal or parallel.

Example: The dog barks but the meowing comes from the kitten.

The dog barks but the kitten meows.

1. I went on vacation to Spain, but my sister went to England for her vacation._____

   _____

2. Olive is very tall, and she is playing basketball. _____

   _____

3. The dog barked all night so the cat is hiding. _____

   _____

4. The train traveled quickly, but it does not make it on time to the next stop. _____

   _____

5. The gift is not for you, nor will I give it to Sheila. _____

   _____

6. The cupcakes were delicious and tasting the cookies is divine. _____

   _____

7. Alex has blue eyes and hair that is brown._____

   _____

8. The playground is full of children, but empty was the cafeteria._____

   _____

9. The book is good, but it was long. _____

   _____

WRITE ON!

On a separate sheet of paper, write two sentences using parallel phrasing. Compare and contrast two different activities. How are the activities alike? How are they different? Exchange papers with a classmate. Have the classmate underline the parallel phrasing used in each sentence.

Name _____ Date _____

Coordinating Conjunctions

A **coordinating conjunction** joins words to words, phrases to phrases, and sentences to sentences. The words joined together are equal or of a similar type. Each coordinating conjunction has a different use. Coordinating conjunctions include the following words:

and—joins two similar ideas

but—joins two contrasting ideas

for—to explain the first part of the sentence

nor—a negative expression

or—shows an alternative idea

so—the second idea (part of the sentence) is a result of the first idea (part of the sentence)

yet—like the conjunction *but*, it joins two contrasting ideas

PRACTICE

Use a coordinating conjunction to complete each sentence.

Example: I like seafood *but* not squid.

1. Dr. Margo has a great talk show, _____ it is on too late for me to watch.

2. The airplane took off on time, _____ it landed early.

3. Ruben forgot his homework, _____ he did not get his recess.

4. Brittany is a great dancer, _____ she cannot sing.

5. Do you like the Bulls _____ the Bears?

6. The celebrity appears down to earth, _____ in reality he is very demanding.

7. Jake drew a picture, _____ Mom hung it on the refrigerator.

Draw a line through any incorrect conjunctions. Write the correct conjunction above the line.

Matt has always dreamed of owning a new car. He has always wanted a Mars Sports Car. He has the accessories all picked out. He wants air conditioning, a CD player, an alarm system, and not a sunroof. All summer he worked hard but saved his money. By the end of the summer, he had enough money to buy the sports car, yet he did!

WRITE ON!

On the back of this page, write about a time you worked hard and saved your money to buy something important. What did you buy? Why? Use at least three coordinating conjunctions and underline them in the paragraph.

Name _____ Date _____

Coordinating Conjunctions

A **coordinating conjunction** connects words in a sentence. Coordinating conjunctions include *for, and, nor, but, or, yet, so, because, since.*
No comma is needed when using a coordinating conjunction to join two words.

    Example: I like bread *and* butter for snack.

Use a comma before the conjunction when joining two independent clauses.

    Example: Taylor lost the hammer, but Elise lost the nails.

Add a coordinating conjunction to each sentence.

    Example: Her skin is dry <u>and</u> rough.

1. Craig cleaned windows _____ washed dishes to earn extra money.

2. Do you live in Crown Heights _____ Happy Valley?

3. The brownstone _____ the neighborhood have a lot of charm.

4. The weather is dreary _____ drab in the winter.

5. Martha likes the dress, _____ it is too expensive.

6. Do you want to be an insurance agent _____ a realtor?

7. The club raised money for the library _____ not the computer lab.

8. Would you like soup _____ salad with your meal?

9. He can either go snowboarding, _____ he can go skiing.

10. She had no trouble learning the routine, _____ she was a dancer.

On a separate piece of paper, write a paragraph discussing two activities or sports that you would like to try and two that do not interest you. Use at least four coordinating conjunctions.

Name _____   Date _____

Correlative Conjunctions

Correlative conjunctions always come in pairs. Correlative conjunctions are *either–or, neither–nor, both–and, not only–but also, whether–or, as–as.*

    Examples: Herman can have *either* spinach *or* broccoli.

             He *not only* cleaned his room *but also* swept the porch.

PRACTICE

Underline the correlative conjunctions used in the paragraph.

      My parents gave my brother and me a choice. We could either go to camp or spend the summer with my grandparents. Both my brother and I like camp, and we would get to see all of our old camp buddies. But my brother and I also like to visit my grandparents. My grandparents live in the mountains where it is cool. If we go to camp, we can either sleep in a tent or in a cabin. If we stay with my grandparents, we sleep neither in a tent nor in a cabin. We have to sleep in bunk beds in the house. Not only is this a difficult decision, but also one we don't want to make!

Write a sentence for each pair of correlative conjunctions.

1. (neither–nor) _____

_____

2. (both–and) _____

_____

3. (not only–but also) _____

_____

4. (whether–or) _____

_____

5. (as–as) _____

_____

6. (either–or) _____

_____

Which correlative conjunction would you use to show:

1. Similar ideas? _____

2. Contrasting ideas? _____

WRITE ON!

Have you ever had to choose between two things you really wanted to do? How did you decide? Use a separate sheet of paper to write a paragraph describing the choice you made and how you made it. Use correlative conjunctions in your description. Underline the correlative conjunctions in the paragraph.

Name _____ Date _____

Subject Pronouns

A **pronoun** can replace a noun that is the subject of a sentence.

    Example: Nina has the measles. *She* has the measles.

        The subject pronoun *she* replaces the noun Nina.

A **subject pronoun** tells *who* or *what* about the sentence. *I, you, he, she, it, we,* and *they* are subject pronouns.

    Example: *He* mows the lawn. *He* is the subject pronoun.

Rewrite each sentence replacing the subject with an appropriate subject pronoun.

    Example: *Toby and Gus* are best friends.

        We are best friends. *They* are best friends.

1. Mr. O'Leary works at night at the factory. _____

2. The striped tie was made by a famous abstract artist. _____

3. The yellow team issued a challenge. _____

4. My husband built the dining table and chairs. _____

5. Giselle's hair is really blonde. _____

6. Heath eats breakfast every morning. _____

7. The psychic is unable to predict the future. _____

8. Eva and I are both trying out for the same part in the play. _____

9. Esteban filled his pockets with frogs. _____

10. Dry skin is a common problem during the colder months. _____

On a separate sheet of paper, write a paragraph about what you like to do on rainy days. Rewrite the paragraph replacing the subject nouns with appropriate subject pronouns.

Name _____ Date _____

Object Pronouns

An **object pronoun** is used after an action verb or in a prepositional phrase. Object pronouns *me, you, him, her, it, us, them* can be used as direct objects, indirect objects, or objects of the preposition.

Example: The ball is for *Marie*.   The ball is for *her*.

Who is the ball for? <u>Her</u>   *Her* is the object pronoun used as the object of the preposition "for."

PRACTICE

Underline the direct object, indirect object, or object of the preposition in each sentence. Write an appropriate object pronoun on the line.

Example: Joe passed the test to <u>Tom</u>.   <u>him</u>

1. Ann and Kelly raced in the marathon. _____

2. The blanket was made by Grandma Rose. _____

3. The letters were put in the mailbox. _____

4. The bus picked Callie and me up. _____

5. The final bell rang stopping the game. _____

6. The present is for Mr. and Mrs. Boyd. _____

7. The dog ate the box. _____

8. The rafters paddled down the river. _____

9. The lipstick is not for the baby! _____

10. Put the stamps on the letter. _____

Draw a line through each direct object, indirect object, or object of the preposition in the paragraph below. Write an appropriate object pronoun above the line.

   Every weekend, Garrett gets up early and heads out to the gardening shed. He picks up his tools and then starts to work on the garden. First, he pulls up the weeds. He is careful not to disturb the young seedlings. Then, he hoes the soil to make it easier for the plants to grow. Garrett carefully checks the plants for bugs. Finally, Garrett gives the plants a good drink of water. Garrett cleans the tools and puts the tools away.

WRITE ON!

On a separate sheet of paper, write a paragraph describing the kinds of plants you would grow in your garden. Discuss how your garden is arranged. Make certain to include object pronouns in your paragraph. Underline the object pronouns used in the paragraph.

Name _____   Date _____

Interrogative Pronouns

An **interrogative pronoun** asks a question. Interrogative pronouns include *who, whom, whose, which, what, whoever, whatever, whomever, whenever,* and *whichever.*

Underline the pronouns used as interrogative pronouns in the paragraph below.

     The baker had a busy day ahead. He had to make over a hundred loaves of bread for the banquet. "Where is the flour? I can't find the flour. Ahhh. . . . there it is. What else do I need to make this special bread? I want the person who eats it to think it's the best bread ever." The baker added water to the flour and other ingredients. He began to knead the dough. "Which kind of pan should I use? I could use the heart-shaped pans or just make simple round loaves. Whichever shape I make, I'm sure the guests will love it!"

Write a question for each interrogative pronoun.

     Example: *Whose* jacket is that?

1. *who*— _____

2. *whom*— _____

3. *whose*— _____

4. *which*— _____

5. *what*— _____

6. *whoever*— _____

7. *whatever*— _____

8. *whomever*— _____

If you could interview anyone in the world, whom would you interview? Write a list of questions you would like to ask this person on the back of this page. Underline the interrogative pronouns used in the questions.

Name _____   Date _____

Demonstrative Pronouns

A **demonstrative pronoun** is used in place of a specific noun. The four demonstrative pronouns are *this, those, that, these*. (**Note:** If these words precede the noun instead of replacing it they are demonstrative adjectives, not pronouns.)

     Example: *This* is wonderful. (demonstrative pronoun)
              This food is wonderful. (demonstrative adjective)

Demonstrative pronouns can be singular or plural.

This and *that* are singular demonstrative pronouns.

     Example: *That* was delicious!

These and *those* are plural demonstrative pronouns.

     Example: *Those* were delicious!

A demonstrative pronoun can be the subject of a sentence or the direct object of a sentence.

     Examples:

          These are on sale. (subject)
          I don't like *these*. (direct object)

PRACTICE

Complete each sentence with the correct demonstrative pronoun. In some cases, more than one pronoun will work.

     Example: <u>That</u> really smoothed my rough skin.

1. _____ was scrumptious!

2. Have you seen _____? They sharpen themselves.

3. _____ is an exciting piece of sculpture.

4. _____ are for the rummage sale.

5. _____ is on sale.

6. Ted gave him _____ for his birthday.

7. Kiera wrote a novel about _____.

WRITE ON!

Have you ever had to take care of a rowdy sibling or younger child? Write about the experience on a separate sheet of paper. Use at least three demonstrative pronouns. Underline the demonstrative pronouns used in the paragraph.

Name _____   Date _____

Demonstrative Pronouns

A **demonstrative pronoun** names (points out) a specific noun without naming it. The four demonstrative pronouns are *this, those, that, these.*

     Example: *That* is an expensive piece of furniture.

This and *these* are demonstrative pronouns that refer to nouns that are close in space or time.

     Examples: *This* is the one that I want.   *These* are the ones I want.

That and *those* are demonstrative pronouns that refer to nouns that are further away in space or time.

     Examples: *That* is a great salad.   *Those* are great in salads.

Write a demonstrative pronoun on the line in the sentence. If you chose a pronoun to signify something *close*, place a **C** after the sentence. Place an **F** after the sentence to signify something *further away*.

     Example: I would like to purchase one pound of <u>this</u> cheese. <u>C</u>

  1. Where are _____ going? _____

  2. It is _____ that is causing all of the fence problems. _____

  3. _____ are $2.49 a pound. _____

  4. _____ is the car that almost hit me. _____

  5. We would like to rent _____ for the weekend. _____

  6. What is wrong with _____? _____

  7. What did you think of _____? _____

  8. _____ belong to me. _____

  9. _____ belongs to Kimberly. _____

10. _____ is the best-tasting pizza I have ever had! _____

11. _____ are way too hot! _____

12. Stephanie is perfect for _____! _____

On a separate sheet of paper, write a paragraph describing a favorite object. Explain what makes it so special. Use at least two or three demonstrative pronouns in the paragraph and underline them.

Name _____   Date _____

Possessive Pronouns

A **possessive pronoun** tells who owns the item mentioned or referred to in the sentence.

    Examples: This is *my* book.   This is *their* house.

Singular Possessive Pronouns	Plural Possessive Pronouns
my, mine	our, ours
his, her, hers, its	their, theirs

PRACTICE

Rewrite each sentence using possessive pronouns. Underline the pronouns.

    Examples: This is Grandma's rocking chair.   This is <u>her</u> rocking chair.

           The watch belongs to my dad.   The watch is <u>his</u>.

1. Benny and I have boots and skis in the garage. _____

    _____

2. This is the Ransoms' yard sale. _____

    _____

3. The dolls are Crystal's. _____

    _____

4. Anita's room is always as neat as a pin. _____

    _____

5. Jeff's motorcycle is in tip-top shape. _____

    _____

6. The limousine is for Jane. _____

    _____

7. The paintings were Shelby's. _____

    _____

8. Mary's sunglasses were designed by Sam and Joan. _____

    _____

9. The little boy's bowl is over there. _____

    _____

10. The computer belongs to me. _____

    _____

WRITE ON!

Use a separate sheet of paper to describe your favorite character from a television program. Use at least three possessive pronouns in your paragraph. Exchange papers with a classmate. Have the classmate underline the possessive pronouns.

Name _____   Date _____

Possessive Pronouns

A **possessive pronoun** tells who owns the item mentioned. Apostrophes are not needed with possessive pronouns.

Examples: He broke *his* arm.
              The doctor is in *her* office.

Singular Possessive Pronouns	Plural Possessive Pronouns
my, mine	our, ours
your, yours	your, yours
his, her, hers, its	their, theirs

Underline the possessive pronouns in the paragraph below.

Micha has a new sewing machine. The sewing machine is the newest of its kind. It can embroider, make buttonholes, and do a hundred different stitches. Her machine is much fancier than ours. Its attachments came in a separate box. Micha first saw the sewing machine in a magazine but she had to wait for a year before the machine was actually on the market. Micha proudly put the new sewing machine in her craft room. She can't wait to use it.

Write three sentences. Use a possessive pronoun in each sentence.

1. _____

2. _____

3. _____

Have you ever saved up money from birthdays, allowances, chores, etc., to buy something really special? How did you earn or receive the money? How long did it take you to save enough money? What did you buy? Write a paragraph on a separate sheet of paper describing what you did to save the money and what you purchased with it. Underline the possessive pronouns used in the paragraph.

Parts of Speech

Name _____   Date _____

Indefinite Pronouns

An **indefinite pronoun** does not name or refer to a specific noun. Most indefinite pronouns are singular and take a singular verb.

Examples: *Anybody* can do this problem.

Everything is wrong!

None of my flowers grew.

Indefinite Pronouns			
any	each	few	nothing
anybody	everybody	no one	somebody
anyone	everyone	nobody	someone
anything	everything	none	something

PRACTICE

Underline the indefinite pronoun in each sentence.

Example: <u>Nobody</u> will help me.

1. Was anybody home?

2. Place everything in the trash.

3. Where is everyone?

4. Nothing can be done to help the situation.

5. Can somebody help me?

6. Everybody is either busy or has gone home.

7. No one attended the bingo party.

8. Somebody will find my missing jacket.

Write a sentence for each of the indefinite pronouns.

1. (anyone) _____

2. (any) _____

3. (few) _____

4. (none) _____

5. (anything) _____

6. (each) _____

WRITE ON!

On a separate sheet of paper, write about a time somebody made a mess, ate the last cookie, left fingerprints on the window, or created some other type of problem. Underline the indefinite pronouns used in the paragraph. Try to have at least four indefinite pronouns in the paragraph.

Name _____   Date _____

Reflexive Pronouns

A **reflexive pronoun** refers to the subject in the same sentence. (The subject and the reflexive pronoun refer to the same person or thing.)

Examples: He gave *himself* a bad haircut.   They saw *themselves* to the door after the party.

Underline the reflexive pronoun in each sentence and circle the subject.

Example: (Marcie) made herself a giant sandwich.

1. George saw himself in the mirror.

2. You should let yourself into the house if I am not home.

3. They always treat themselves well.

4. I built this birdhouse myself.

5. The dog chased itself.

6. The boys completed the hard puzzle by themselves.

7. My mom taught the class herself.

8. The cat scared itself when it looked in the window.

9. Mom parked the RV herself.

10. Claire painted herself into a corner.

Underline the reflexive pronouns used in the paragraph.

My dad was trying to do the taxes by himself. He bought a special computer program that was supposed to make doing the taxes easy. Dad read the directions, installed the software, and started to input the information. When he became stuck, he called my mom for help. My mom was busy making herself a snack. My dad called me. I told my dad I was busy cleaning my room. Finally, my dad called the dog. The dog came and ate the directions. My dad hit himself in the head with the box and turned off the computer.

On a separate sheet of paper, write about a time you helped someone do a task. Underline the reflexive pronouns used in the paragraph. Try to use at least three reflexive pronouns.

Subject and Predicate

A complete sentence has both a subject and a predicate. The **subject** contains a noun or a pronoun. The noun or pronoun tells whom or what the sentence is about.

     Example: The doctor is in surgery.

            The subject is *the doctor*.

The **predicate** contains a verb or linking verb. The predicate tells what the subject *did* or what the subject *is*.

     Example: The doctor is in surgery.

            The predicate is *is in surgery*.

Underline the complete sentences.

     Example: <u>Renee enjoys being a pediatric nurse.</u>

1. Some firefighters are also paramedics.
2. A paramedic helps save lives.
3. Some people work as flight paramedics.
4. A flight paramedic.
5. Cares for others.
6. Some nurses work in hospitals.
7. Others work in.
8. Paramedics and nurses receive a lot of training.
9. Sick people.

Draw a box around the subject in each sentence and underline the predicate.

     Example: |They| <u>ordered a pepperoni pizza.</u>

1. He put cheese on his pizza.

2. Bonnie peeled the pepperoni off her pizza.

3. Sammy slid it out of the oven.

4. Theo tossed the dough.

5. The delivery person carried the pizza up the stairs.

6. She and I sprinkled the toppings on the pie.

Write a paragraph on the back of this page describing your favorite kind of pizza. Rewrite the paragraph on a separate sheet of paper. Make two of the sentences incomplete sentences. Exchange papers with a classmate. Have a classmate underline the incomplete sentences.

Subject and Predicate

A complete sentence has both a subject and a predicate. The **subject** contains a noun or a pronoun. The noun or pronoun tells whom or what the sentence is about.

>   Example: The floats were leading the parade.
>
>   The subject is *the floats*.

The **predicate** contains a verb or linking verb. The predicate (verb) tells what the subject did or is.

>   Example: The floats were leading the parade.
>
>   The predicate is *were leading the parade*.

A complete sentence must have subject-verb agreement. If the subject is singular, naming one person, place, or thing, the verb must be singular, too.

>   Example: The *stereo has* a great sound.

If the subject is plural, naming more than one person, place, or thing, the verb must be plural, too.

>   Example: The *stereos have* great sound.

Read the paragraph. Underline the sentences with subject-predicate agreement. Correct the other sentences by crossing out the wrong word and writing the correct word above it.

    Moosie had a litter of puppies. There was ten puppies in the litter. There were six girl and four boy puppies. The biggest puppy were named Piggy. Piggy was twice the size of the other puppies. The smallest puppy were a boy. He liked to sleep on his back. One of the puppies was named Lightning because his white patch of fur looked like a streak of lightning. Another puppy have a white patch of fur that looked like a flame.

Rewrite each sentence so that there is subject-verb agreement.

1. The ladder need to be moved. _____
2. The paint are still wet. _____
3. Has you ever been to the zoo? _____
4. There is dogs next door. _____
5. Chief, my dog, escape all the time. _____

Should animals be kept in a zoo? Why or why not? Use a separate sheet of paper to write a paragraph on this topic and share your opinion with the class. Reread your paragraph and make certain your subjects and predicates are in agreement. Underline the subjects *once* and the predicates *twice*.

Name _____   Date _____

Subject and Predicate

A complete sentence has a **subject** describing whom or what the sentence is about and a **predicate** telling what the subject did. A complete sentence also has subject-predicate agreement. In subject-predicate agreement, the noun and verb must agree in number (either singular or plural).

Example: We are going to the movies.
We is the subject.
Are going to the movies is the predicate.
We is a plural pronoun and *are going* is a plural linking verb. This sentence has subject-predicate agreement.

PRACTICE

Read each sentence. Change each sentence from a singular subject-predicate agreement to a plural subject-predicate agreement.

Example: The glass is on the table.   The glasses are on the table.

1. The computer is on the fritz again.

   _____

2. The boy loves the little dog.

   _____

3. The science-fiction movie is earning rave reviews.

   _____

4. The cherry pie is cooling on the counter.

   _____

5. The manager of the store was very friendly.

   _____

Read the word groupings below and decide whether the subject or the predicate is missing. Use the phrases to write complete sentences with subject-predicate agreement.

6. the old man and woman

   _____

7. traveled to a new planet

   _____

8. wondered at the stars

   _____

WRITE ON!

On a separate sheet of paper, write four sentences with mistakes in each sentence—no subject, no predicate, or no subject-predicate agreement. Exchange papers with a classmate. Have the classmate rewrite each sentence correctly.

Name _____   Date _____

Declarative Sentences

There are four types of sentences: *declarative, interrogative, imperative*, and *exclamatory*.

A **declarative sentence** is a statement of fact or opinion. A declarative sentence begins with a capital letter and ends with a period.

Examples: I had an appointment this morning.   The car is blue with black trim.

Use *proofreading marks* to correct each sentence. Place three small lines under each letter that should be capitalized in the sentence. Add the appropriate punctuation to the end of each sentence. Circle periods added to be certain they are noted.

Example: A name is just a name.

1. walter does not work very often

2. everything adds up to twelve

3. the author finished writing the book

4. mr. stucky is getting married

5. cheryl runs up and down the stairs for exercise

6. robin and dave host a weekly talk show

7. the movie was pretty spooky

8. the chocolate flower tasted delicious

9. the clock beeps every half hour

10. mrs. davis bought a new washer and dryer

Use proofreading marks to correct the paragraph. Draw a line through any incorrect word. Write the correct word above the line.

Josiah were trying out for the school's chess team. He have to play a chess match against the team's coach, ms. Warner   josiah made the opening move. Soon, Ms. Warner and Josiah was locked in battle   the chess match ended in a draw. Josiah became the newest member of the chess team.

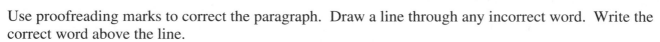

What do you know about the game of chess? On a separate sheet of paper, write a paragraph on the topic. Rewrite the paragraph omitting several capital letters and periods. Exchange papers with a classmate. Use proofreading marks to correct the mistakes.

Name _____ Date _____

Declarative Sentences

A **declarative sentence** is a statement of fact or opinion. A declarative sentence begins with a capital letter and ends with a period.

Example: Jeremy went to the mountains for the weekend.

Write a declarative sentence about each topic.

Example:

watermelon—In the summer months I like eating nice, juicy slices of watermelon.

1. ostriches— _____

_____

2. trees— _____

_____

3. tractors— _____

_____

4. cell phones— _____

_____

5. rulers— _____

_____

Cross out the sentences in the paragraph that are not declarative sentences.

Have you ever been mountain climbing? It's a wonderful sport, lots of fun, and great exercise. Before you go out mountain climbing, it is best to take a class. You are probably wondering, "Where do I go to take a mountain climbing class?" Well, you might check at a local health club, adult school, or nearby college. The class will train you in the basics of mountain climbing and will probably take you out to a nearby mountain to test your newly-developed skills. Why should people bother to take a class? After all, most people know how to climb trees. Mountain climbing is completely different than tree climbing. In mountain climbing there are not any tree branches to grasp or stand on or anyone nearby to call for help. To climb some types of mountains, you need special equipment and training. Why not go ahead and give it a try? You will be glad that you did.

On a separate sheet of paper, write about a new sport that you would like to try. What makes the sport seem interesting to you? Do you need any special training or equipment? Use at least four declarative sentences.

Name _____   Date _____

Interrogative Sentences

An **interrogative sentence** asks a question. An interrogative sentence begins with a capital letter and ends with a question mark.

Example: Why is Betty complaining so much?

PRACTICE

Rewrite each sentence using the correct punctuation.

1. when is it going to rain_____

_____

2. why is Benita always late for work _____

_____

3. why was the mummy wrapped in cloth _____

_____

4. have you ever been to Egypt _____

_____

5. do the Johnsons live in the two-story house_____

_____

6. did the wind blow the table over _____

_____

7. what caused the building to collapse _____

_____

8. how is calculus different from geometry _____

_____

Many questions begin with interrogative pronouns. The interrogative pronouns are *who, whom, whose, which, what, whoever, whatever, whomever,* and *whichever*. Write questions below using three of these interrogative pronouns.

1. _____
2. _____
3. _____

WRITE ON!

Pretend you are conducting an interview. Whom would you interview? What questions would you ask? Write five possible interview questions on the back of this page. Try to use different interrogative pronouns.

Name _____   Date _____

Interrogative Sentences

An **interrogative sentence** asks a question. An interrogative sentence begins with a capital letter and ends with a question mark.

> Examples: Did Noah finish reading the book?
>
> Will the boat be leaving at dawn?

PRACTICE

Rewrite each declarative sentence as an interrogative sentence.

> Example: Aimee left her jacket in the classroom.
>
> Where did Aimee leave her jacket?

1. Marie takes a vitamin every morning.

   _____

2. Wilbur wants to be a detective when he grows up.

   _____

3. Dad decided to grow a beard.

   _____

4. Chartreuse is her favorite color.

   _____

5. The furniture store had a spring sale.

   _____

6. The name of the new school is Fremont Elementary.

   _____

7. They named the baby Madeline Marie.

   _____

8. Europe is home to many royal families.

   _____

9. Cherise creates magnificent pieces of silver jewelry.

   _____

10. The book is on the bestsellers' list again.

   _____

11. Marcus was wearing a garish purple tie.

   _____

12. Ivan does not like to brush his teeth.

   _____

WRITE ON!

On the back of this page, make a list of five questions you would ask an Olympic athlete. Check to make sure each interrogative sentence begins with a capital letter and ends with a question mark.

Name _____   Date _____

Imperative Sentences

An **imperative sentence** is a command or an order. An imperative sentence begins with a capital letter and ends with a period. In an imperative sentence, the subject (you) is not used. It is understood that you are the recipient of the command.

    Examples: Go put on a coat.   Wash your hands.   Stand by the door.

PRACTICE

Rewrite each declarative or interrogatory sentence as a command.

    Example: Virginia washes the dishes after dinner.

             Wash the dishes.

1. Hank does his homework every night.

    _____

2. Walter was careful with his lunch money.

    _____

3. Lauren does not eat candy.

    _____

4. Will you paint the deck?

    _____

5. You need to pack your bags for the trip.

    _____

6. Will you watch your little brother?

    _____

7. We asked Josie to walk the dogs.

    _____

8. Would you write a letter to Great Aunt Myrtle?

    _____

9. Susie makes the best lemonade.

    _____

10. Would you stop making that squeaking noise?

    _____

WRITE ON!

On a separate sheet of paper, write a paragraph on a topic of your choice. Rewrite the paragraph, using only imperative sentences. Which paragraph do you think is more interesting to read?

Name _____   Date _____

Imperative Sentences

An **imperative sentence** is a command or an order. An imperative sentence begins with a capital letter and ends with a period. In an imperative sentence, the subject (you) is not used. It is understood that you are the recipient of the command. Imperative sentences are used when giving directions, sharing a recipe, or writing the rules.

Examples: Turn left at the corner.

Stop at the stop sign.

Pour one cup of flour into the bowl. Add the rest of the wet ingredients. Stir well.

PRACTICE

Write three of your school or classroom rules using imperative sentences.

1. _____

_____

2. _____

_____

3. _____

_____

Write the steps for making your favorite snack using imperative sentences.

Step 1. _____

Step 2. _____

Step 3. _____

Step 4. _____

Step 5. _____

Step 6. _____

WRITE ON!

On a separate sheet of paper, write directions to get from school to your home. Use imperative sentences when writing the directions.

Name _____   Date _____

Exclamatory Sentences

An **exclamatory sentence** shows strong emotion. An exclamatory sentence begins with a capital letter and ends with an exclamation point.

Example: Randall won the election!

Read each sentence. Decide which sentences are exclamatory (E) and which are declarative (D). Place an E or a D at the beginning of each sentence. Add exclamation points to the end of exclamatory sentences and periods to the end of declarative sentences.

Example: ___E___ Mom had sextuplets ___!___

_____   1. Deidre went to the grocery store _____

_____   2. Tina went to the movies _____

_____   3. The bank is being robbed _____

_____   4. Lionel parked the car _____

_____   5. Blair won the New York Marathon _____

_____   6. Geoffrey read a book _____

_____   7. We won the Liberty Bowl _____

_____   8. I am so mad _____

_____   9. Wolfie took his first steps _____

_____   10. The ship is sinking _____

_____   11. The sky is falling _____

_____   12. The fence was painted white _____

_____   13. We can build a fire in the fireplace _____

_____   14. The dogs are napping under the tree _____

_____   15. I can't find the baby _____

On a separate sheet of paper, write about going to an auction and winning the bid for something very special. Use at least one exclamation point in your paragraph.

Name _____   Date _____

Types of Sentences

There are four types of sentences: *declarative, interrogative, imperative*, and *exclamatory*.

A **declarative** sentence is a statement of fact or opinion. A declarative sentence begins with a capital letter and ends with a period.

An **interrogative** sentence asks a question. An interrogative sentence begins with a capital letter and ends with a question mark.

An **imperative** sentence is a command or order. An imperative sentence begins with a capital letter and ends with a period. The subject (you) is understood, not written.

An **exclamatory** sentence shows strong emotion. An exclamatory sentence begins with a capital letter and ends with an exclamation point.

Read each sentence. Determine which type of sentence it is and label the sentence on the line provided beside the sentence. Rewrite each sentence on the line below, using capital letters and ending punctuation where appropriate.

Example: take your seats—<u>Imperative</u>

    <u>Take your seats.</u>

1. don't look at your neighbor's paper _____

_____

2. who studied for this test _____

_____

3. raise your hand _____

_____

4. mario earned the highest score _____

_____

5. the test has twenty questions _____

_____

6. are you ready _____

_____

7. write your name at the top of the paper _____

_____

WRITE ON!

Write an example of each type of sentence on the back of this page, but don't add the punctuation. Exchange papers with a classmate. Have the classmate add the correct ending punctuation and label the type of sentence.

Types of Sentences

There are four types of sentences: *declarative, interrogative, imperative*, and *exclamatory*.

Examples:

Declarative: I went to the store.   **Imperative:** Go to the store.

Interrogative: Are you going to the store?   **Exclamatory:** I don't want to go to the store!

Read each sentence and identify which type it is on the line.

Example: Follow the rules.   <u>Imperative</u>

1. Can you follow the recipe? _____

2. I can't find my lucky rabbit's foot! _____

3. Use wood glue for this project. _____

4. Where are the drawing pencils? _____

5. I found a treasure map! _____

6. I want to see the new pirate movie. _____

7. The cat is licking its paws. _____

8. This is the best brownie ever! _____

9. Are you allergic to walnuts? _____

10. What is your favorite kind of exercise? _____

11. The Crookshanks have traveled to India. _____

12. I got the movie star's autograph! _____

13. I have bingo! _____

14. Make the baby stop crying. _____

15. Drink plenty of water each day. _____

16. Did you eat everything in your lunch? _____

17. Where did Mavis leave her cell phone? _____

18. Why did you borrow my camera? _____

19. Gerry swept the sidewalk. _____

20. The weeds are growing in the flower beds. _____

WRITE ON!

On a separate sheet of paper, write a paragraph on a topic of your choice. Use one example of each kind of sentence in the paragraph.

Name _____   Date _____

DAILY
Warm-Up 60

Types of Sentences

A **declarative sentence** is a statement of fact or opinion. A declarative sentence begins with a capital letter and ends with a period.

An **interrogative sentence** asks a question. An interrogative sentence begins with a capital letter and ends with a question mark.

An **imperative sentence** is a command or order. An imperative sentence begins with a capital letter and ends with a period.

An **exclamatory sentence** shows strong emotion. An exclamatory sentence begins with a capital letter and ends with an exclamation point.

PRACTICE

Rewrite each paragraph adding the correct capital letters and ending punctuation to each sentence.

Paragraph 1

    my shoes are killing my feet   what was I thinking   i should have listened to my mom   she wanted me to get something sensible, like sneakers   instead, i bought the mile-high platforms   never again

_____

_____

_____

_____

Paragraph 2

    in the middle of the night, we awoke to a weird ringing sound   where was the ringing coming from   mom checked in the bathroom   dad checked in the garage   my sister and i looked in the living room   finally, mom found what was making the ringing noise   it was the kitchen timer   guess where mom found the timer   it was in her purse

_____

_____

_____

_____

WRITE ON!

On a separate sheet of paper, write a paragraph on a topic of your choice. Try to use each of the four types of sentences. Share your paper with a classmate and check each other's work.

Name _____ Date _____

DAILY
Warm-Up 61

Dependent Clauses

A **dependent clause** contains a subject and a verb. By itself, a dependent clause is not a complete sentence. Use a comma after a dependent clause at the beginning of a sentence. Often, but not always, a dependent clause begins with one of the following words or phrases: *after, although, because, before, even though, since,* or *when.*

> Example: Even though it is hot, people still like to sunbathe.
>> The dependent clause is *Even though it is hot.*

Use a comma before and after the dependent clause that is in the middle of a sentence.

> Example: Quilting, which is an American tradition, is still popular today.
>> The dependent clause is *which is an American tradition.*

No comma is needed if the dependent clause is at the end of the sentence.

> Example: The wallpaper began peeling from the wall before the day was over.
>> The dependent clause is *before the day was over.*

PRACTICE

Underline the dependent clause in each sentence. Add commas where needed.

> Example: <u>When working with fire</u>, one needs to be careful.

1. After the game was over the people exited the stadium.

2. When he lost out on the story the news reporter threw a temper tantrum.

3. The fire engine which is made in Germany is the best one made.

4. The forest which is filled with many living things is a beauty to behold.

5. When you finish the test you can put it in the basket.

Underline the dependent clauses in the paragraph.

> Grandpa always likes to tell stories about his youth. "When I was your age, I had to walk to school fifteen miles through sleet and snow. Then, on the way home, I had to walk uphill 20 miles." We always wondered how that was possible, but we never asked him. "When I was knee-high to a grasshopper, I had to milk one hundred cows and feed the horses out in the pasture." We thought that was odd because Grandpa grew up in the city. "Way back when, I had to catch fish with my bare hands and then eat it raw." Grandpa's parents owned a grocery store when he was young. As you can see, our Grandpa is quite a storyteller!

WRITE ON!

Do any of your family members tell tall tales? On a separate sheet of paper, write a paragraph about one of the tall tales. If you can't recall any family tall tales, make one up! Include at least three dependent clauses in your paragraph.

Name _____ Date _____

Independent Clauses

An **independent clause** contains a subject and a predicate. An independent clause is a complete sentence. The predicate always contains the verb and the words following it.

> Example: It started raining.
> The subject is *It*.
> The predicate is *started raining*.

Underline the independent clauses.

> Example: Even though it rains, <u>the mail carriers still deliver the mail.</u>

1. I will call you when your order is ready.

2. When it is time to go, put on your shoes.

3. Sherry makes her bed before going to school.

4. The alarm rings whenever the wind blows hard.

5. Because of the dust storm, the windows are filthy.

6. Whenever he studies for a test, Barnaby does really well.

7. While walking at night, Garth fell into the shallow end of the pool.

8. Because they used the same glass, all of the kids came down with chicken pox.

9. The tree grew tall and strong despite being in a shady area.

10. Whenever he smells bacon, the dog gets so excited.

11. Whenever it snows, we put on our snowsuits and go out and play.

12. Despite losing the game, the team was in good spirits.

Write two independent clauses.

1. _____

2. _____

What is the difference between an independent clause and a dependent clause?

_____

_____

Pretend you are going on a safari. What would you take and why? Write a paragraph on a separate sheet of paper about your adventure. Underline the independent clauses used in the paragraph.

Name _____   Date _____   DAILY Warm-Up 63

Dependent and Independent Clauses

A **dependent clause** can have a subject and a verb, but it is not a complete sentence by itself. It does not express a complete thought.

Examples: when I am sad   while the snow is falling   if I get taller

An **independent clause** has a subject and a verb. It is a complete sentence by itself.

Examples: I like to watercolor.   The ground is hard.

Identify the underlined part of each sentence as a *dependent* or *independent* clause.

Example: <u>When visiting Argentina</u>, remember to dance with the locals.   <u>dependent</u>

1. <u>The storm passed over the town</u> before it hit the next city. _____

2. While in the candy shop, <u>Rhea tasted many delicious samples</u>. _____

3. Before starting the car, <u>check to make sure there is nothing behind it</u>. _____

4. <u>Despite being extremely old</u>, the truck ran like a charm. _____

5. <u>While jogging around the block</u>, Melody found a little puppy. _____

Underline the dependent clauses in the paragraph.

 Douglas owns many vending machines which are located throughout the valley. Each day at dawn, he gets in his truck. He spends the day servicing and refilling the machines. At each machine, Douglas fills up any empty slots and collects the money. Douglas also checks to make sure each machine has plenty of change to give to the customers who pay with dollar bills. Douglas' final stop of the day is the bank, where he deposits the day's receipts. When he returns home, Douglas restocks his truck with the necessary food items.

Write a dependent clause.

_____

Write an independent clause.

_____

Have you ever bought anything from a vending machine? How did the machine work? What did you buy? Write a paragraph on a separate sheet of paper describing your experience. Underline the dependent clauses used in the paragraph.

Complex Word Families

A **word family** is a set of rhyming words with the same simple endings.

    Example: *-at*—bat, cat, hat, fat

A **complex word family** might have a vowel pair, a consonant blend, or both, as an ending spelling.

    Example: *-ight*—fight, tight, light, bright

PRACTICE

Write one or more meanings for each word in the *-etch* and *-aunt* complex word families. Use a dictionary, if necessary. Tell whether it is a noun (n.), a verb (v.), or an adjective (adj.).

1. stretch: _____

2. wretch: _____

3. sketch: _____

4. ketch: _____

5. fetch: _____

6. haunt: _____

7. flaunt: _____

8. jaunt: _____

9. daunt: _____

10. gaunt: _____

Complete the paragraph using the words from above.

    My Great-Aunt Flavia visited recently. She had gotten very thin. She looked

_____, but was excited to be traveling. The journey was a pleasant _____

for her to make by train. She used to live here and sail on her father's _____. She wanted

to visit her favorite _____, the Olde Soda Shoppe. I told her it had been torn down to

make room for a new shopping mall. She was sad because she used to sit in one of the booths and

_____ the nearby scenery.

WRITE ON!

Have you ever been given a daunting task? What was the task? Did you succeed? Use a separate sheet of paper to write about the experience. If you can't think of one, make one up.

Name _____ Date _____

Complex Word Families

A **complex word family** might have a vowel pair, a consonant blend, or both, as an ending spelling.

 Examples: *-ough*—rough, tough

     -ouse—house, mouse, louse

Use the Word Bank and a dictionary, if necessary, to write the word that fits each definition.

Word Bank			
-inge		*-ought*	
binge	hinge	bought	ought
cringe	tinge	brought	sought
fringe	twinge	fought	thought

1. _____ : a small stab of pain

2. _____ : past tense of bring

3. _____ : to eat a lot of food at one time

4. _____ : to seek out (past tense)

5. _____ : to shy away in fear or pain

6. _____ : an idea

7. _____ : allows a door to open and close

8. _____ : should do something

9. _____ : past tense of fight

10. _____ : past tense of buy

Use the Word Bank to complete the paragraph.

 After Tommy was hit by the ball, he felt a _____ of pain in his side. He

_____ out the team doctor for help. When the doctor took out a needle, Tommy began to

_____. Tommy was scared just by the _____ of getting a shot. When the

doctor saw that Tommy's face was a _____ green, she put the needle away.

On a separate sheet of paper, write a paragraph using at least three words from one of the complex word families in the Word Bank.

Vocabulary

Name _____   Date _____

Complex Word Families

A complex word family is a set of rhyming words with a more difficult ending spelling. A complex word family might have a vowel pair, a consonant blend, or both, as an ending spelling.

Examples: *-oan*—moan, groan, loan

PRACTICE

Word Bank						
-aught		*-ound*			*-ould*	
caught	haughty	around	flounder	pound	could	
daughter	naughty	bound	ground	round	should	
fraught	taught	expound	hound	sound	would	
		found	mound			

Use the words in the Word Bank to complete each sentence. Cross out each word as you use it.

Example: Dad loves to <u>expound</u> on that topic!

1. Did you hear that _____?

2. I _____ the class how to crochet.

3. Paul _____ do it if he wanted to.

4. Uncle Bob _____ the limit on fish.

5. We went to the _____ to get a dog.

6. There is a _____ of dirty clothes on the floor.

7. My _____ studies ballet.

8. _____ you like to order dessert?

9. The Wallaces' took a cruise _____ the world.

10. The dog _____ a bone in the backyard.

11. The hot air balloon touched down on the _____.

12. The _____ won Best in Show.

13. Grapes, oranges, and apples are all _____ in shape.

WRITE ON!

On a separate sheet of paper, write a paragraph using the remaining words in the Word Bank.

Homophones

Homophones are two or more words that sound the same but have different spellings and different meanings.

Examples: *I*–referring to oneself   *aye*–meaning "yes"   *eye*–used to see with

Use homophones from the box to the right to complete each sentence.

Example: There was a <u>beech</u> tree growing near the <u>beach</u>.

1. My _____ used to have a small _____ farm.
2. In _____ weather, the _____ take to the coop.
3. Grandpa will give a _____ when he sees how much you have _____.
4. The old _____ will _____ tirelessly through the thick mud.
5. The _____ truck ran over the lady's big _____.
6. He will play the _____ of the buttered _____ in the Thanksgiving play.
7. There is a _____ growing in the _____ of plants.
8. _____ wiped his feet on the door _____.
9. The cleaner stood on the _____ of the ladder and _____ out the sponge.
10. _____ you be able to replicate this chest made from _____?
11. Do _____ see the _____ in the pasture?
12. Farther down the _____, there is a _____ station for large trucks.
13. The coins were _____ from the king's _____.
14. I, _____, have _____ siblings who go _____ that school.
15. Aubrey _____ the package for one _____.
16. Alex found the _____ at the garage _____.

Homophones
aunt—ant
boar—bore
foul—fowl
groan—grown
Matt—mat
role—roll
rose—rows
rung—wrung
sail—sale
sent—cent
thrown—throne
too—two—to
tow—toe
way—weigh
would—wood
you—ewe

Make a list of homophones on the back of this page. Use several of the homophones in a sentence.
Exchange papers with a classmate. Have the classmate underline the homophones used in the paragraph.

Name _____ Date _____

Homophones

Homophones are two or more words that sound the same but have different spellings and different meanings.

Examples: *male*—a man   *mail*—a letter or magazine delivered to one's home

PRACTICE

Use each pair of homophones in a sentence.

Example: (your/you're) You're your dog's favorite playmate!

1. scent/sent:_____

2. know/no:_____

3. we/wee: _____

4. hair/hare: _____

5. break/brake: _____

6. in/inn: _____

7. sun/son: _____

8. capitol/capital: _____

9. ate/eight:_____

10. cell/sell: _____

Complete each sentence with the correct pair of homophones.

The father and _____ woke up with the rising _____.
The _____ of bacon _____ them rushing to the dining hall. At
_____ in the morning, they _____ breakfast down in the dining room.
After leaving the _____, they both got _____ the golf cart and headed
down to the lake. Soon, Junior said, "Did you see that track in the mud? I wonder if it belongs to a
bear!" "Now, son. Don't let your imagination get away from you. You _____ there are
_____ bears in this area!"

WRITE ON!

Homophones can be confusing. Do you have any tips or tricks to know which word to use? If you do,
write them on the back of this page. If you do not, write two sentences using pairs of homophones.

Name _____ Date _____

Homophones (our, hour)

Homophones are two or more words that sound the same but have different spellings and different meanings.

> Examples: *Our* is a possessive pronoun—Our parents like to go hiking.
>
> *Hour* refers to time—At what hour does the party start?

PRACTICE

Complete each sentence with the correct word, *our* or *hour*.

1. _____ school has the highest test scores in the entire state!

2. Where is _____ homeroom teacher?

3. _____ class never has perfect attendance.

4. In an _____, the assembly will start.

5. It took him more than an _____ to walk two laps!

6. The game will last about an _____.

7. _____ family has a pet chicken named Wilbur.

8. There are 60 minutes in one _____.

9. It felt like an eternity, but it was really only an _____.

10. _____ city is known for its delicious seafood!

11. Do you know what _____ state flower is?

12. Will the movie last more than an _____?

Complete the paragraph with the correct homophones.

   At a certain _____ , _____ family likes to go hunting for fireflies. As soon as it is dark outside, we are ready to go. My sister and I get to stay up more than an _____. _____ grandparents grab the glass jars and _____ parents are armed with butterfly nets. We have such a good time!

WRITE ON!

If you had one hour to do anything you wanted with your family, anything in the world, what would you do with that one hour? Write a paragraph on a separate sheet of paper sharing your wish. Use the homophones *our* and *hour* in your paragraph.

Name _____   Date _____

Homophones (there, their, they're)

Some **homophones** cause confusion, such as: *there, their,* and *they're*. How do you know which one to use?

> **They're** is a contraction for **they are**.
> > Example: They're playing a game.

Break the contraction apart into two separate words, *they are,* and reread the sentence. They are playing a game.

> **Their** shows ownership.
> > Example: Their house is two blocks over.

Substitute another pronoun that shows ownership, such as *my*. My house is two blocks over.

> **There** shows location.
> > Example: There is my backpack.

Substitute another location word to see if the sentence will work. Here is my backpack.

PRACTICE

Write the correct word—*there, their,* or *they're*—on the line.

1. _____ always on time for dinner.

2. Fred left his skateboard over _____ by the tree.

3. _____ favorite hobby is playing lacrosse.

4. _____ dog, the black and white spotted one, is only three months old.

5. _____ are ten girls and eight boys in my class.

6. _____ team is wearing orange shirts and yellow helmets.

7. _____ participating in the Civil War re-enactment this weekend.

8. Where is _____ car?

9. Is _____ a gas station on the next street?

10. _____ next in line.

Write a sentence for each homophone—*there, their,* and *they're*.

1. _____

2. _____

3. _____

WRITE ON!

On a separate sheet of paper, write a paragraph using *there, their,* and *they're*. Have a classmate check your use of each of the homophones.

Name _____ Date _____

Homophones (to, too, two)

There are some **homophones** that cause confusion, such as: *two*, *too*, and *to*. How do you know which one to use?

Two—is a number word.　　**To**—means *in the direction of*.　　**Too**—means *in addition to* or *also*.

　　Example: I ate *two* cookies.　　Example: I gave this *to* you!　　Example: I was at the party, *too*.

Write the correct word—*two*, *too*, or *to* on the line.

1. _____ people showed up for the all-you-can-eat buffet.

2. Most people have _____ legs.

3. If you want to go, _____, you need to ask your parents.

4. My sister wanted to go, _____.

5. The dentist pulled _____ teeth before putting my braces on.

6. I went _____ the store with my mother.

7. My brother, Ed, ate _____ many donuts for breakfast.

8. My mom has _____ sisters and one brother.

9. I would like _____ be an only child!

10. Mr. Zenno gives _____ many tests!

11. The P.E. teacher had us skip _____ times and then hop three times.

12. Dr. Thompson has _____ offices in town.

13. Alice can multiply up _____ the sixes.

14. Gil is not allowed _____ play with Justin.

15. Have you ever been _____ the Monterey Bay Aquarium?

Write a sentence for each homophone— *two*, *too*, and *to*.

1. _____

2. _____

3. _____

On a separate sheet of paper, write a paragraph using the three homophones featured above. If you need a topic for your paragraph, use the suggestion below.

　　What if everything in the world came in two's—two desks, two computers, two houses, two plates, two friends, etc. Describe what the world might be like.

Homographs

Homographs are words with the same spelling but different meanings and sometimes different pronunciations.

Example: *angle*—to fish with a hook and line; a shape formed by two connected lines.

Read the whole sentence to determine the correct meaning and pronunciation of the word.

Example: *ball*—a fancy dance; a spherical object

Each year, the governor throws a *ball* for all of her supporters.

In this sentence, a *ball* is a fancy dance.

PRACTICE

Write two meanings for each word. Use a dictionary to help you.

Example: band—a strip of fabric used to hold items together or a group of musicians

1. squash—_____

   _____

2. ring—_____

   _____

3. page—_____

   _____

4. mum—_____

   _____

5. quack—_____

   _____

6. stable—_____

   _____

7. bank—_____

   _____

8. yen—_____

   _____

9. spruce—_____

   _____

10. pump—_____

    _____

WRITE ON!

On a separate sheet of paper, write a paragraph using several homographs. Exchange papers with a classmate. Have the classmate underline the homographs used in the paragraph.

DAILY
Warm-Up 73

Homographs

Homographs are two words with the same spelling but different meanings.

   Example: *sink*—to go under water; used to wash dishes in

Read the whole sentence to determine the correct meaning of the homograph.

   Example: *bed*—a place to sleep; a place to plant flowers

      In the springtime, the beds will be alive with daisies.

      In this sentence, *beds* is a place to plant flowers, not a place to sleep.

PRACTICE

Write the meaning of the underlined homograph on the line. Use a dictionary if needed.

   Example: The <u>slug</u> crawled slowly along the sidewalk.

      <u>A slug is a slow-moving plant pest.</u>

1. The <u>roots</u> have caused the sidewalk to buckle and crack.

   _____

2. The <u>pitcher</u> threw the ball as hard as she could and struck the batter out.

   _____

3. Sit here for the <u>present</u> time.

   _____

4. The <u>school</u> swam this way and that way through the cool ocean water.

   _____

5. Put the pigs in the <u>pen</u>.

   _____

6. Use the answer <u>key</u> to correct the papers.

   _____

7. The dog always sits on Grandma's <u>lap</u>.

   _____

8. The <u>well</u> has run dry.

   _____

WRITE ON!

On a separate sheet of paper, write a paragraph describing the parts of a tree. Many of the parts are homographs. How many can you include? Underline the homographs used in the paragraph.

Name _____   Date _____

Heteronyms

Heteronyms are words that are spelled the same but have different meanings and different pronunciations.

   Examples: *bass*—a type of fish   *bass*—a low voice

PRACTICE

Use a dictionary. Write two different meanings for each word. Use a dictionary to help you. Choose meanings that cause the words to be pronounced differently.

1. bow _____

   bow _____

2. tear _____

   tear _____

3. desert _____

   desert _____

4. close _____

   close _____

5. dove _____

   dove _____

6. minute _____

   minute _____

7. object _____

   object _____

WRITE ON!

On a separate sheet of paper, write a paragraph on a topic of your choice. Try to use several heteronyms in the paragraph. Exchange papers with a classmate. Have the classmate underline the heteronyms used in the paragraph.

Heteronyms

Heteronyms are words that are spelled the same but have different meanings and different pronunciations.

Examples: *refuse* (n.)—garbage
refuse (v.)—to say no

Write the meaning for the underlined heteronym.

Example: When painting wood, use a good <u>primer</u> as a first coat.

primer: a special type of paint used to cover unpainted wood.

1. I <u>object</u> to having a cemetery built next to the school.

   _____

2. Please <u>record</u> the contestants' names and the order of their appearance.

   _____

3. The results were <u>invalid</u> and the votes had to be recounted.

   _____

4. Do not <u>tarry</u> in the morning.

   _____

5. The <u>wind</u> is blowing the leaves in all directions.

   _____

6. Each morning, I <u>wind</u> my watch.

   _____

7. Shawn broke the snowboarding <u>record</u>.

   _____

Underline the pair of heteronyms used in each sentence. Read the sentences aloud to hear the different pronunciations.

1. In the spring, the sow will sow her seeds.

2. After a loud row with her husband, the wife decided to row her boat across the lake.

3. The sewer dropped her garment into the sewer.

4. I felt a tear in my eye after I began to tear the onion apart.

5. The minute snail traveled an inch per minute.

On a separate sheet of paper, write a paragraph using two pairs of heteronyms. Read the sentences to a classmate so that the different pronunciations are clear.

Analogies

An **analogy** shows the relationship between two items. When completing an analogy, first determine the relationship between the first pair of words. Are they opposites? Are they similar? Do they show change over time? The second pair of words must have the same relationship as the first pair of words.

Example: puppy : dog :: kitten : cat

This is read as "puppy *is to* dog *as* kitten *is to* cat."

The relationship shows change over time—*a baby animal to adult animal.*

PRACTICE

Complete each pair of analogies.

Example: arm : (is to) leg :: (as) finger : (is to) toe

1. left : right :: day : _____

2. eye : see :: nose : _____

3. bracelet : wrist :: ring : _____

4. boy : girl :: man : _____

5. button : shirt :: zipper : _____

6. soap : hands :: shampoo : _____

7. soup: hot :: ice cream : _____

8. cut : bandage :: break : _____

9. water : tub :: potting soil : _____

10. socks : feet :: gloves : _____

11. watch : time :: _____ : weight

12. open : close :: _____ : empty

13. stove : cook :: _____ : bake

14. cat : meow :: _____ : bark

15. bird : nest :: _____ : den

WRITE ON!

On the back of this paper, write three analogies for a classmate to complete. Trade papers and, if there is time, work together to come up with more analogies.

Vocabulary

Name _____   Date _____

Analogies

An **analogy** shows the relationship between two items. When completing an analogy, first determine the relationship between the first pair of words. Are they opposites? Are they similar? Do they show change over time? The second pair of words must have the same relationship as the first pair of words.

    Example: up : down :: left : right

           This is read as "up *is to* down *as* left *is to* right." The relationship shows opposites.

PRACTICE

Complete each pair of analogies. Identify the relationship.

    Example: tire : round :: box : <u>square</u>   <u>items and their shapes</u>

	Analogy	**Relationship**
1.	plane : fly :: boat : _____	_____
2.	Mexico : Spanish :: France : _____	_____
3.	movie : watch :: music : _____	_____
4.	ice cream : cold :: coffee : _____	_____
5.	ruler : inch :: scale : _____	_____
6.	penny : one cent :: quarter : _____	_____
7.	three : four :: nineteen : _____	_____
8.	cow : milk :: chicken : _____	_____
9.	adobe : mud :: igloo : _____	_____
10.	penguin : swims :: eagle : _____	_____
11.	bee : hive :: wasp : _____	_____
12:	camera : film :: printer : _____	_____
13.	eyes : eyeglasses :: ears : _____	_____
14.	cheese : dairy :: bread : _____	_____
15.	farm : domesticated :: zoo : _____	_____

WRITE ON!

Write a paragraph on a separate sheet of paper. Use one of the analogy pairs above to establish your topic.

Synonyms

Two or more words in the same language with the same or similar meaning are called **synonyms**.

A thesaurus is a writer's tool. It is a book listing synonyms. Each entry word is in alphabetical order. It tells the part of speech and lists the synonyms for the word. A thesaurus does not offer definitions but instead provides other words that could be used in place of the word being researched.

In a *thesaurus,* the word "cute" would be listed as—**cute** *adj.*, attractive, pretty

In a *dictionary,* the word "cute" might be listed as—**cute** *adj.*, attractive in a pretty way

PRACTICE

Use a thesaurus to find two synonyms for each word.

Example: like <u>fancy, enjoy</u>

1. say   _____ , _____
2. awesome   _____ , _____
3. pretty   _____ , _____
4. won   _____ , _____
5. color   _____ , _____
6. friend   _____ , _____
7. play   _____ , _____
8. game   _____ , _____
9. pig   _____ , _____
10. book   _____ , _____

Use synonyms to replace the underlined words. Rewrite the paragraph on a separate sheet of paper.

My <u>friend</u> and I decided to <u>try</u> a new game. The game was called Be a Pig! To win, your <u>pig</u>
   1   2   3
needs to be the first one to <u>eat</u> everything in the trough. First, each player <u>picks</u> a pig and places it at the
                              4   5
trough filled with yarn loops. Then, each player uses the pig's snout to pick up as many yarn loops of

the same <u>color</u> without dropping any. When all of the loops have been picked up, the players say, "Oink!
          6
Oink!" and count their loops.

1. _____   3. _____   5. _____
2. _____   4. _____   6. _____

WRITE ON!

Write a list of synonyms for the word *mistake* on a separate sheet of paper. Then, write a paragraph using as many of them as you can to discuss a mistake you once made.

Synonyms

Two or more words in the same language with the same or similar meaning are called **synonyms**. A thesaurus is a reference book filled with synonyms and occasionally antonyms (opposites). For each word listed, the part of speech is given, followed by a list of alternative words for the entry.

  Example: **jewelry** *noun*,–adornment, embellishment

PRACTICE

Rewrite each sentence replacing the underlined word with a synonym. Use a thesaurus if needed.

  Example: Last night, I had a <u>horrible</u> dream.

      Last night, I had a <u>terrible</u> dream.

1. I dreamed that a <u>monster</u> was chasing me.

   _____

2. I jangled my keys as I <u>walked</u> to my motorcycle.

   _____

3. I rode quickly down the <u>street</u>.

   _____

4. I <u>hit</u> the horn to warn people about the danger.

   _____

5. The monster <u>stomped</u> down the street behind me.

   _____

6. It kept <u>growling</u> at me.

   _____

7. I <u>crashed</u> my motorcycle.

   _____

8. I landed face-first in a <u>blob</u> of wet cement.

   _____

9. When I woke up, I had my pillow <u>stuffed</u> in my mouth.

   _____

10. What a <u>crazy</u> dream!

   _____

WRITE ON!

On a separate sheet of paper, write a paragraph using two pairs of synonyms. Have a classmate find the synonyms and underline them.

Vocabulary

Name _____ Date _____

Antonyms

Two words with opposite meanings are called **antonyms**.

A thesaurus is a writer's tool that can be used to find antonyms, as well as synonyms. Each entry word provides the part of speech followed by the synonyms for the word. It then lists any antonyms possible for the word.

Example: **baby** n., infant, toddler ANT: adult

PRACTICE

Use a thesaurus to find an antonym for each word.

Example: close <u>distant</u>

1. able _____
2. restore _____
3. sell _____
4. timid _____
5. ugly _____

6. sad _____
7. responsible _____
8. tidy _____
9. contempt _____
10. excitable _____

Replace each underlined word with an antonym and rewrite the paragraph.

Howie has <u>many</u> great talents. One of them is his amazing ability to <u>remember</u> people's names. A <u>girl</u> taught him this important skill. <u>She</u> told Howie to look a <u>new</u> acquaintance in the eye. Then, <u>whisper</u> the person's name three times in the conversation.

_____

_____

_____

_____

_____

WRITE ON!

On a separate sheet of paper, write a paragraph about a great day. Replace the positive words used in the paragraph with their antonyms. Reread both paragraphs. Which day sounds more exciting?

©Teacher Created Resources, Inc.   87   #3995 Daily Warm-Ups: Language Skills

Synonyms and Antonyms

Two words with similar meanings are called **synonyms**.

  Example: student—pupil

Two words with opposite meanings are called **antonyms**.

  Examples: detect—conceal old—new

For each word, write a synonym and an antonym. If you need help, use a dictionary or a thesaurus.

  Example: *funny*—synonym: <u>amusing</u> antonym: <u>humorless</u>

Word	Synonym	Antonym
1. swallow (v.)	_____	_____
2. random (adj.)	_____	_____
3. separate (v.)	_____	_____
4. private (adj.)	_____	_____
5. elastic (n.)	_____	_____
6. content (adj.)	_____	_____
7. mediocre (adj.)	_____	_____
8. frugal (adj.)	_____	_____
9. deform (v.)	_____	_____
10. coarse (adj.)	_____	_____
11. traitor (n.)	_____	_____
12. comical (adj.)	_____	_____

On a separate sheet of paper, write a paragraph on a topic of your choice. Underline three words in the paragraph that could have an antonym or a synonym. Exchange papers with a classmate. Have the classmate rewrite the paragraph replacing the underlined words with synonyms or antonyms.

Synonyms and Antonyms

Two words with similar meanings are called **synonyms**.

     Example: *work* and *toil* are synonyms

Two words with opposite meanings are called **antonyms**.

     Examples: *work* and *play* are antonyms and <u>toil</u> and <u>play</u> are antonyms

PRACTICE

Look at the word pairs and determine if they are *antonyms* or *synonyms*.

     Example: benefit—advantages <u>synonyms</u>

1. outrage—anger   _____

2. gigantic—minute   _____

3. brazen—shameless   _____

4. scold—chastise   _____

5. praise—criticize   _____

6. hazardous—safe   _____

7. beautiful—hidious   _____

8. gaudy—tasteless   _____

9. restrain—activate   _____

10. borrow—return   _____

11. shackle—hamper   _____

12. argument—quarrel   _____

13. sure—uncertain   _____

14. teach—learn   _____

Rewrite the paragraph using synonyms for the underlined words.

     Today I went to <u>see</u> the latest action movie, *Spider Pig*. It was a nice movie. Spider Pig had a red, white, and blue <u>costume</u>. He could climb <u>tall</u> buildings and swing through the air like a <u>big</u> spider. Spider Pig saved the girl pig from the <u>mean</u> Mad Hog Scientist. It was a good movie.

_____

_____

_____

_____

WRITE ON!

On the back of this sheet, make a list of five descriptive words you use too often. Next to each overused word, write a synonym that can be used in its place. Can you think of antonyms for the words as well?

Latin Word Origins

Many of the words we use every day have **Latin origins**. If the meaning of the Latin root is known, the meaning of the entire word can be determined.

> Example: The Latin root *aptus* means *suitable*—What does the word *aptitude* mean in the following sentence?
>
> She has a great *aptitude* for playing the piano.
>
> Meaning: The ability to play the piano well. *She is suited to play the piano.*

PRACTICE

Determine the meaning for the underlined word in each sentence. Rewrite the sentence to include the meaning of the underlined word. Clues are provided using the Latin roots of the words. If you need more help, use a dictionary.

> Example: *Voc* is derived from the Latin root for *voice*.
>
> Vincent is an <u>advocate</u> for children's rights.
>
> Meaning: <u>Vincent is a voice for children and their rights.</u>

1. **volv**—to roll; to change

Over time, fish have <u>evolved</u> to become the creatures we see today.

Meaning: _____

2. **serv**—save or keep

We must do everything we can to <u>preserve</u> the forest for future generations.

Meaning: _____

3. **orig**—beginning

In the <u>original</u> film, the villain got away.

Meaning: _____

4. **migr**—change or move

During the cold winter months, many birds <u>migrate</u> to warmer climates.

Meaning: _____

5. **numer**—number

There are <u>numerous</u> books on that specific topic.

Meaning: _____

6. **loc**—place

Margie <u>dislocated</u> her shoulder playing softball.

Meaning: _____

WRITE ON!

On a separate piece of paper, use two or three words with Latin roots (from above) to write a paragraph. Exchange papers with a classmate. Have the classmate underline the Latin root words used in the paragraph. Can you list other words having the same root?

Latin Word Origins

Many of the words we use every day have **Latin origins.** If the meaning of the Latin root is known, the meaning of the entire word can be determined.

    Example: *Lab*—*work*
              We will <u>collaborate</u> on this project.
              Meaning: <u>We will work together.</u>

Determine the meaning for the underlined word in each sentence. Rewrite the sentence to include the meaning of the underlined word. Clues are provided using the syllables derived from Latin roots of the words. If you need more help, use a dictionary.

    1. *form*—shape; not changing

At many schools the students are required to wear <u>uniforms</u>.

Meaning: _____

    2. *narr*—to tell

The <u>narrator</u> has an important part in the play.

Meaning: _____

    3. *man*—hand

The <u>manuscript</u> tells the story of the Civil War.

Meaning: _____

    4. *ques*—to ask or to seek

Joey is full of <u>questions</u>!

Meaning: _____

    5. *pop*—people

Our city has a growing <u>population</u>.

Meaning: _____

Underline the words in the sentences below that use the Latin origins above.

    1 Despite popular opinion, the Senator will not run for office again.
    2. The author had many requests for public appearances.
    3. The narrative tells the story from the Mother's point of view.
    4. The company manufactures many items made from plastic.
    5. For true reform to take place, there must be true acceptance.

Use a separate sheet of paper to write a paragraph using as many variations of the root *ques* as you can. Underline the words.

Name _____ Date _____

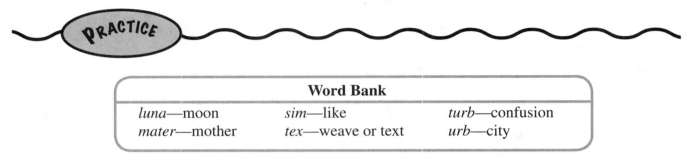

Latin Word Origins

Many of the words we use every day have **Latin origins**. If the meaning of the Latin root is known, the meanings of the entire word can be determined.

Example: **act**: meaning *do*—*act*ion, *act*or, re*act*, trans*act*, en*act*

PRACTICE

Word Bank		
luna—moon	*sim*—like	*turb*—confusion
mater—mother	*tex*—weave or text	*urb*—city

Underline the words with the Latin roots above. Write the meaning of the word on the line.

Example: During a <u>luna</u>r eclipse, the moon cannot be seen. <u>an eclipse of the moon</u>

1. The pilot said we might hit some turbulence. _____

2. The twins look very similar._____

3. On which floor is the maternity ward?_____

4. Many families live in the suburbs. _____

5. In the southern states, there are many textile manufacturers. _____

6. I love the texture of that fabric! _____

7. Simultaneously, they both shouted out the answer!_____

8. Tonight, there will be a lunar eclipse. _____

9. My sister put a "Do not disturb" sign on her door. _____

10. In the urban areas, housing can be very expensive. _____

11. My sister is very maternal._____

12. Similes compare two things using the words *like* or *as*. _____

WRITE ON!

Use a separate sheet of paper to write a paragraph using one of the Latin root words. Use as many forms of the word as possible in your paragraph. A dictionary may be helpful. Exchange papers with a classmate. Have the classmate underline the Latin root words used in the paragraph.

Name _____   Date _____

Greek Word Origins

Many of the words we use every day have **Greek origins**. If the meaning of the Greek root is known, the meanings of the entire word can be determined.

Example: ***aero***—*air* aerobics, aerodynamics

Aerodynamics is the study of air and solid bodies moving through it.

PRACTICE

Word Bank		
biblio—book	*cardio*—heart	*photo*—light
bio—life	*phob*—fear	*therm*—heat

Underline the words with Greek roots in the sentences below. Write the meanings of the words on the lines at the ends of the sentences. You may need a dictionary, too!

Example: Remember to include the <u>bibliography</u> at the end of the report.   <u>list of books used</u>

1. The photographer took all of our wedding pictures. _____

2. When Ray grows up, he would like to be a biologist. _____

3. If you have arachnophobia, that means you are scared of spiders! _____

4. Amy always keeps her coffee in a thermos. _____

5. My mom used a telephoto lens to get a close-up of the polar bear and her cubs. _____

6. Irene is extremely claustrophobic. _____

7. I can't find the thermometer! _____

8. Abraham Lincoln was a great bibliophile. _____

9. My grandpa went to see the cardiologist today. _____

10. During the cold winter months, Paul wears thermal underwear. _____

Underline the different forms of the Greek root *therm* used in the paragraph below.

Gilbert dressed warmly. He put on his thermal underwear, followed by his heavy snowsuit. He poured hot chocolate into his trusty thermos and tightened the lid. Before leaving the house, he checked the temperature on the thermometer. It was 0 degrees. He decided it was too cold to go outside. He turned the thermostat up to a toasty 70 degrees and snuggled under a blanket to watch the news.

WRITE ON!

Use a separate sheet of paper to write a paragraph using one of the Greek root words suggested above. Use as many forms of the word as possible in your paragraph. A dictionary may be helpful. Exchange papers with a classmate. Have the classmate underline the Greek root words used in the paragraph.

Name _____ Date _____

Greek Word Origins

Many of the words we use every day have **Greek origins**. If the meaning of the Greek root is known, the meanings of the entire word can be determined.

> Example: *agri* means *field*
>
> The valley is known for its *agricultural* products.
>
> What does *agricultural* mean? *Agricultural* refers to items grown in the field.

Determine the meaning for the underlined word in each sentence. Rewrite the sentence to demonstrate the meaning of the underlined word. If you need help, use a dictionary.

> Example: *Ortho* is derived from the Greek word for *straight*.
>
> I have been going to the <u>orthodontist</u> for a year.
>
> Meaning: <u>I have been seeing a dentist that straightens teeth.</u>

1. **Onym** is derived from the Greek word for *name*.

   Write three <u>synonyms</u> for this word.

   Meaning: _____

2. **Mech** is derived from the Greek word for *machine*.

   The <u>mechanic</u> is a genius!

   Meaning: _____

3. **Meter** is derived from the Greek word for *measure*.

   How long is a <u>centimeter</u>?

   Meaning: _____

4. **Geo** is derived from the Greek word for *earth*.

   My favorite subject in school is <u>geography</u>.

   Meaning: _____

5. **Gram** is derived from the Greek word for *written*.

   People used to receive <u>telegrams</u>.

   Meaning: _____

Underline the words with Greek roots in the sentences below.

1. My mom is always nagging me about using correct grammar.
2. The thermometer is in the medicine cabinet.
3. The door opens with a secret mechanism.
4. What grade did you get on the geometry test?
5. What is the antonym for *loud*?

On a separate sheet of paper, write a paragraph using words from the Greek roots provided on this page. Underline the words with Greek roots used in the paragraph.

Name _____ Date _____

DAILY Warm-Up 88

Greek Word Origins

Many of the words we use every day have **Greek origins**. If the meaning of the Greek root is known, the meanings of the entire word can be determined.

    Example: *agri* means *field*

        The valley is known for its *agricultural* products.

        What does *agricultural* mean? Items grown in the field.

PRACTICE

Determine the meaning for the underlined word in each sentence. Use a dictionary if you need more help.

    Example: **Opt** is derived from the Greek word for *eye*.

        My <u>optician</u> is Dr. George.

        Meaning: <u>Dr. George is an eye doctor.</u>

1. **Chron** is derived from the Greek word for *time*.

    List the events in <u>chronological</u> order.

    Meaning:_____

2. **Cycl** is derived from the Greek word for *cycle*.

    Many towns are devastated by <u>cyclones</u>.

    Meaning:_____

3. **Ast** is derived from the Greek word for *star*.

    The <u>astronaut</u> is scared and excited about flying into space.

    Meaning:_____

4. **Log** is derived from the Greek word for *word*.

    Make sure you <u>apologize</u> after hurting someone.

    Meaning:_____

5. **Dont** is derived from the Greek word for *tooth*.

    When Gregory grows up, he wants to be an <u>orthodontist</u>.

    Meaning:_____

Underline the words with Greek roots and give a possible meaning on the line provided.

1. What is a chronometer? _____

2. Orthodontics is a fascinating topic. _____

3. The store sells many different kinds of bicycles._____

WRITE ON!

Use a separate sheet of paper to write a paragraph using as many variations of the root *cycl* as you can. Underline the words.

Name _____   Date _____

Prefixes (un-, re-, pre-, dis-)

A **prefix** is a word part (syllable) added to the beginning of a root or base word. A prefix changes the meaning of the word. Sometimes it can change the word root to its opposite.

Example: *un*+happy=unhappy (not happy)

PRACTICE

Prefix Word Bank			
dis- opposite of	*pre-* before	*re-* again	*un-* not

Underline the word with a prefix. Write the meaning of the word on the line next to the sentence.

Example: Margie has to <u>redo</u> the assignment. <u>to do again</u>

1. Moe is unable to help us during the carnival. _____

2. Were you able to preview the movie? _____

3. Why do you distrust her? _____

4. The clocks are preset to go off at the same time! _____

5. The keys will unlock all of the doors. _____

Write a word with a prefix for each definition.

1. To not like _____   6. To view again _____

2. To wind again _____   7. To pay before _____

3. To test again _____   8. To not be assembled _____

4. To assemble again _____   9. To not like the taste _____

5. To appear again _____   10. To tie again _____

Read the paragraph. Underline the words with prefixes. Circle the base words.

Mack decided to buy a rebuilt model train for his collection. He knew it had been repackaged but didn't know he would have to reassemble it himself. Mack took the model home only to discover there were about a million pieces to this model train! The pieces came presorted by shape. Instead, Mack sorted the pieces by size, and then resorted them by color. Finally, Mack was ready to start assembling the pieces. After his first attempt the train didn't look right, so he disassembled the train and put it together a different way. It still didn't look right, so Mack decided to box up the train and return it for a train that came preassembled!

WRITE ON!

On a separate sheet of paper, write a paragraph using four words that have prefixes. Share the paragraph with a friend, and see if he or she can underline all the words with prefixes.

Prefixes (in-, en-, fore-)

A **prefix** is added to the beginning of a root or base word. A prefix changes the meaning of the word. Often, a prefix changes the definition of the base word to its opposite.

Example: *in* + action = inaction (no action)

PRACTICE

Prefix Word Bank
en- in, into, to put into   *in-* no, not   *fore-* before, in front of

Underline the word with a prefix on each line. Write the meaning of the word on the line next to the sentence.

Example: Roger is <u>incapable</u> of telling the truth.   <u>Not able to</u>

1. Dr. Bill wrote the foreword for this latest bestseller. _____

2. Be forewarned. It is a hard test. _____

3. The homework assignment was incomplete. _____

4. Hillary was the forerunner in the election. _____

5. Our supply budgets are inadequate for our needs. _____

6. That boy is incapable of writing a complete sentence. _____

7. She claims to be able to foretell the future. _____

8. Do not encroach upon the hermit's space. _____

9. We will encode this computer program. _____

10. The wedding is going to be an informal event. _____

Write a word with a prefix for each definition. Underline the prefix.

1. To not be animated _____

2. Not articulate _____

3. To warn before _____

4. Not adequate _____

5. To close in on _____

WRITE ON!

On a separate sheet of paper write a paragraph about something unusual or magical. Use at least three words with prefixes in your paragraph. Trade papers with a classmate and find each other's prefix words.

Prefixes (pro-, post-, pre-)

A **prefix** is added to the beginning of a root or base word. A prefix changes the meaning of the word.

> Example: The word "pose" can mean *to suggest*. By adding "pro" to the beginning *pro*+pose, the word *propose* is formed. *Propose* means to put forward an idea for consideration.

PRACTICE

Prefix Word Bank
post-after   *pre*-before   *pro*-in favor of

Underline the word with a prefix. Write the meaning of the word on the line.

> Example: The salesman said we could <u>postdate</u> the check.   <u>put a later date on the check</u>

1. This dress predates the Civil War. _____

2. I want to promote healthier eating at school. _____

3. Did you follow the preoperative directions? _____

4. The farmer prohibits using pesticides on his vegetables. _____

5. The counselor gave me a postpaid envelope. _____

6. The soldier was given his ribbons posthumously. _____

7. You can return the cell phone in the prepaid envelope. _____

8. What is the probable outcome of this experiment? _____

Underline the words with prefixes used in the paragraph.

   At the magic show premiere, the magician walked through the audience. He was shaking hands and promoting his movie, *Postscript to a Rabbit*. He promised people tickets to a local preview of the movie. During the show, he called people up to the stage. He gave them all a posthypnotic suggestion. Every time the people heard the word "helium" they were to stand up and start dancing like chickens. It was a great show!

WRITE ON!

Use a separate sheet of paper and choose one of the sentences above to begin a paragraph. Include at least three more words with prefixes in the paragraph. Ask a classmate to underline all the prefix words.

Name _____ Date _____

Prefixes (super-, extra-, intra-)

A **prefix** is added to the beginning of a root or base word. A prefix changes the meaning of the word.

  Example: *super*: more than, above, over, more

      extra: beyond

      intra: within; on the inside

PRACTICE

Use the prefix definitions provided above to write definitions for the words listed below. Use a dictionary if additional help is needed.

  Example: supermarket: more than a market; large grocery store

  1. superhuman: _____

  2. supernatural: _____

  3. intragroup: _____

  4. superfine: _____

  5. intramural: _____

  6. extracurricular: _____

  7. superstar: _____

Select three of the words above to use in sentences.

  1. _____

   _____

  2. _____

   _____

  3. _____

   _____

Underline the words with prefixes used in the paragraph.

  The Visalia Vikings were hosting the local intramural sports teams. The teams came to participate in an extraordinary opportunity. The event was held in the superdome with seating for about 20,000 people! The event was sponsored by the local supermarket and the local superstar, Gladiator Jones. Gladiator Jones was once a sports hero and had participated in extracurricular sports at the local high school. All had a great time!

WRITE ON!

On a separate sheet of paper, write a paragraph describing what it would be like to have superpowers. Try to have at least three words with prefixes in the paragraph.

Name _____ Date _____

Suffixes (-ful, -ly, -er)

A **suffix** is a syllable added to the end of a word. Sometimes the root-word ending changes to accommodate the suffix. For example, when adding *-er* to a short vowel word, double the final consonant before adding the *-er*. (swim + *er* = swimmer—a person who swims)

PRACTICE

Word Bank		
-er—person who_____	*-ful*—full of_____	*-ly*—how it is done

Write the meaning of the words created by adding a suffix to a root word.

Example: driver: person who drives

1. joyful:_____

2. gardener: _____

3. wonderful: _____

4. badly: _____

5. graceful: _____

6. rider:_____

7. teacher:_____

8. weekly:_____

9. hateful: _____

10. safely:_____

Underline the root word once and the suffix twice. Write the meaning of the word on the line.

1. The singers sang the song with enthusiasm and expression. _____

2. Junie grabbed a handful of popcorn to eat during the movie. _____

3. "When I grow up, I want to be a dancer," said Peter. _____

4. Gently tap the bottom of the bread to see if it is done. _____

5. The lawyer won the case for his client. _____

6. The skater did a fantastic routine! _____

WRITE ON!

On a separate sheet of paper, write about what it might be like to be a pet groomer or a groomer for zoo animals. Use at least three words with suffixes in your paragraph and underline them.

Name _____ Date _____

Suffixes (-ible, -able)

A **suffix** is added to the end of a word. A suffix changes the meaning of the word.

Use -*able* if the rest of the word can stand alone as a word.

    Example: reason + *able* = reasonable (*reason* is a word by itself)

Use -*able* if it follows a vowel.

    Examples: agree + *able* = agreeable (*agree* ends in a vowel) note + able = noteable (*e* is dropped)

Use -*ible* if the root is not a complete word.

    Example: vis + *ible* = visible (*vis* is not a word on its own)

PRACTICE

Cross out the word spelled incorectly. Write the correct spelling of the word on the line.

1. Patricia thinks she is quite fashionible/fashionable in her purple and pink dress.

    _____

2. The molecule is not visible/visable to the naked eye. _____

3. Tiffany is a very capible/capable photographer. _____

4. I had a horrible/horrable dream last night. _____

5. A terrible/terrable thing happened to Steve last night. _____

6. It is advisible/advisable to take the detour to avoid possible mudslides.

    _____

7. The judge is an honorible/honorable woman. _____

8. To be suitible/suitable for school, your shorts must touch your knees.

    _____

9. Are mushrooms edible/edable? _____

10. That is the most unbelievible/unbelievable tale I have ever heard! _____

11. Larry is a dependible/dependable worker. _____

12. That was an incredible/incredable save! _____

13. Terry is carrying an unbearible/unbearable workload. _____

14. The house is in a very desirible/desirable location. _____

15. Are those shoes comfortible/comfortable? _____

WRITE ON!

On a separate sheet of paper, write a paragraph describing the most incredible thing you have seen or experienced. What made it so amazing? Use at least two words with suffixes in your paragraph and underline them. Share your paper with a classmate.

Ending Patterns (-age, -edge, -idge)

The soft j sound /j/ at the end of a word can be spelled three different ways: *-age*, *-edge*, or *-idge*.

Use the Word Bank to find a word that fits each clue.

Word Bank		
-idge bridge ridge	*-edge* dredge pledge hedge wedge ledge	*-age* manage sage page stage rage wage

1. to become very angry: _____

2. used to cross a river: _____

3. a group or row of shrubs growing closely together: _____

4. a sheet of paper: _____

5. actors stand on this when performing plays: _____

6. a very wise person; a spice; or a color: _____

7. to stand on the flat surface of a cliff: _____

8. a bumpy surface: _____

9. to clean out the bed of a body of water: _____

10. to promise: _____

Underline the words in the paragraph that have a soft /j/ sound and fit the ending pattern.

Last night, I went to the refrigerator looking for something to take the edge off of my hunger. I looked on the bottom shelf, and I found a wedge of cheese. I put the cheese on a plate. I kept looking, and I did manage to dredge up some old crackers. I used the crackers to make a bridge going across the cheese. I pledged, from then on, to always eat my dinner!

On a separate piece of paper, write a paragraph using words from the Word Bank above. Underline the words you used. Try to use at least five of the words. When you have finished, share your passage with a classmate.

Name _____   Date _____

Ending Patterns (-tion, -sion)

A **word ending** that sounds like "shun" can be spelled *-tion* or *-sion*.

Example: *Attention* class, while I explain the *suspension* policy.

PRACTICE

Word Bank			
action	fraction	nation	section
collection	invention	permission	sensation
confusion	mansion	production	vacation
extension	motion	question	vision

Complete each sentence using the correct word from the Word Bank.

Example: To open the lock, you need to remember the <u>combination</u>.

1. In all of the _____, I lost my backpack.

2. On my summer _____, I went to a ranch in Montana!

3. What _____ of the pizza did you eat?

4. "Do you have a _____?" asked Mrs. Herman.

5. To go on the field trip, all of the students need to have a signed _____ slip.

6. When the movie director said, "_____," all of the actors started speaking.

7. Annie became sick because of the boat's rocking _____ .

8. The tire plant's _____ is up to full speed.

9. Which _____ of the stadium do you want to sit in?

10. Who came up with this useful _____?

11. Swimming in a pool of salt water can be a strange _____.

12. The Grays live in the_____ at the end of the street.

13. Raise your hand if you need an _____ for your book report.

14. I have 20/20 _____.

15. The auto-club provides _____-wide service.

16. Gracie has quite a _____ of bugs!

WRITE ON!

On a separate sheet of paper, write a paragraph about a vacation you would like to take. Use at least four words from the Word Bank above. Underline all the words in your paragraph that end in *-tion* or *-sion*. See if you can add a few that are not on the list.

Name _____ Date _____

DAILY
Warm-Up 97

Frequently Misspelled Words

Some words are frequently misspelled. It takes practice to spell them correctly. It helps to know the correct pronunciation and to read a lot to notice when some words are misspelled.

Examples: *alot* is actually two words and should be written—**a lot**

separate should be spelled—**separate**

calandar has an "e" in the middle syllable and should be spelled—**calendar**

PRACTICE

Write the correct spelling of each word below. Use a dictionary to check your answers and then write the word again. When you have finished, exchange papers with a classmate and quiz each other on the correct spellings.

Example: <u>skedule</u>   <u>schedule</u>

1. ninty   _____   _____

2. fourty   _____   _____

3. temprature   _____   _____

4. theries   _____   _____

5. wierd   _____   _____

6. thier   _____   _____

7. sinse   _____   _____

8. sholder   _____   _____

9. liberry   _____   _____

10. freind   _____   _____

11. lisense   _____   _____

12. allright   _____   _____

13. belive   _____   _____

14. neice   _____   _____

15. nabor   _____   _____

WRITE ON!

Is it important to spell words correctly? Why? On a separate sheet of paper, write a paragraph explaining the importance of good spelling. If possible, give an example of a misspelling that could cause a problem.

Name _____ Date _____

Frequently Misspelled Words

Some words are often misspelled. It helps to keep lists of words you know you misspell and practice writing them. It also helps to use a dictionary and learn about root words, suffixes, and prefixes.

Examples: *mispell* actually has two *s's*—**misspell**

baloon has two *l's* and should be spelled—**balloon**

PRACTICE

Underline the misspelled word in each sentence. Write the misspelled word correctly on the line.

Example: <u>Thay</u> always lose the equipment at recess. <u>They</u>

1. Jeb was not very greatful for all of the help he was given. _____

2. The fire truck is eqipt with many special firefighting features. _____

3. Garth and David's arguement went on and on and on. _____

4. Justin has a poor attitud towards school. _____

5. Do you know how do devide? _____

6. Taylor read nine stores to the kindergartners. _____

7. Which dessert is your favrite? _____

8. This is truely a momentous occasion! _____

9. Stop making such redikulus comments about your sister! _____

10. If you two don't stop talking, I will have to separate you! _____

11. Have you tried the new restrant? _____

12. Remember to yeld to pedestrians. _____

Underline the 10 misspelled words in the paragraph. Write the words correctly on the lines.

I went to the supermarket wif my frend, Stacy. We pickt out several delishus looking vegetables and some tastey fruit. At the cashier's, we payd the clerk and packt our groseries ourselves. We will make some grate tasting kabobs for desert tonight!

1. _____   6. _____
2. _____   7. _____
3. _____   8. _____
4. _____   9. _____
5. _____   10. _____

WRITE ON!

Which is better to use—spell check or a dictionary? Why? Explain your choice on a separate sheet of paper.

Frequently Misspelled Words

Sometimes we misspell words we use every day. It takes practice to become a good speller. It helps to read, too. The more you read and see words in print, the easier it is to recognize when words are spelled correctly.

> Example: pensil—it sounds right when sounded out but "pensil" is actually spelled with a
> soft *c*–**pencil**.

Underline the misspelled words in each paragraph below. Write the misspelled words correctly on the lines following the paragraph.

Paragraph 1

    Finaly, we saw the moving truck comeing down the street. The truck was more than fourty minutes late. We carryied all of our cloths to the truck and the movers loaded up all of our boxes. We were redy to move to our new house!

1. _____   4. _____

2. _____   5. _____

3. _____   6. _____

Paragraph 2

    My famly wanted to start its own business. We could not decide whether to open an entertainment busness, a sports business, or a restrant. We finally realized we were ment to own a dog-walking business. We all love to exrcise and we all love dogs. It is a perfect mach!

1. _____   4. _____

2. _____   5. _____

3. _____   6. _____

On a separate sheet of paper, write three different sentences. Misspell a word or two in each sentence and ask a classmate to find and correct the misspelled words. Talk about the words you often misspell. Perhaps your classmate has a hint to remember how to spell those words.

Name _____ Date _____

Frequently Misspelled Words

Some frequently used words tend to be misspelled.

    Example: *reces* is actually spelled **recess.**

PRACTICE

Miranda wrote a letter to her grandmother. Underline all of Miranda's spelling errors.

> May 21, 2004
>
> Deere Grandma,
>
>   I studyied realy hard on this week's spelling test. I only mist one word! Kan you believe it!
> I mispeld "mowntan." I don't no how I culd hav misspelled that word. I am such a good spelr!
>
>   Next week I will stude even harder and I know I will git 100%.
>
>   Love, Miranda

Write the misspelled words correctly on the lines.

  1. _____
  2. _____
  3. _____
  4. _____
  5. _____
  6. _____
  7. _____
  8. _____
  9. _____
10. _____
11. _____
12. _____
13. _____

WRITE ON!

What can Miranda do to improve her spelling? On a separate sheet of paper, write a paragraph giving
Miranda some spelling tips and hints.

Name _____ Date _____

Syllables

Knowing how to divide a word into **syllables** can help in decoding a new word. Every word has at least one syllable and every syllable must have one vowel sound.

Syllabication Rules

Rule 1: Divide a word between two middle consonants—but never split up digraphs (*th, sh, ph, ch, wh*). Examples: *but-ter sup-pose with-out tel-e-phone weath-er*

Rule 2: Divide a word before a single consonant with a beginning long vowel sound. Examples: *e-ject   u-ten-sil*

Rule 3: Divide a word before the consonant + *le*. Examples: *pur-ple rip-ple*

Rule 4: Divide a word between compound words, prefixes, and suffixes. Examples: *book-mark   re-mark   mark-ing*

PRACTICE

Divide each word into its syllables. Write the word under the correct rule.

Word	Rule 1	Rule 2	Rule 3	Rule 4
Example: into	in-to			
1. shipyard				
2. dreamy				
3. open				
4. bedspread				
5. pillow				
6. flowers				
7. middle				
8. parcel				
9. bathtub				
10. simple				

WRITE ON!

On a separate sheet of paper, write five words with more than one syllable. Trade papers with a classmate and have him or her divide the words into syllables. Check the rules.

Name _____   Date _____

Multiple Meaning Words

A word with more than one meaning is a **multiple meaning word**. The same word can be used as a noun or as a verb.

Example: nursery

I will *nurse* you back to health. (nurse–v. to care for)

Susie is a *nurse* in this hospital. (nurse–n. person who cares for the sick)

PRACTICE

Select the word from the Word Bank that can be used to complete both sentences.

Word Bank								
buckle	guard	picture	pinch	plug	school	squash	touched	wax

1. The candle is made from _____.

   _____ the furniture before you set the table.

2. The _____ marches back and forth in front of the palace.

   The police officers will _____ the priceless treasure.

3. Do you like _____?

   Go _____ that giant pillow!

4. Don't forget to _____ your seatbelt.

   I won this belt _____ at the rodeo.

5. The _____ on the lamp was bent.

   Do not _____ up the sink with the vegetables.

6. The _____ of fish were swimming in the clear, blue water.

   Beverly goes to _____ every day.

7. She felt the _____ as the drawer closed on her fingers.

   The crab will _____ with its front claws.

8. The baby _____ her nose with her toes.

   I was _____ by his generosity.

WRITE ON!

Use a separate sheet of paper. Think of two words with multiple meanings. Create two pairs of sentences leaving a blank space for one of the multiple meaning words. Have a classmate complete each pair of sentences using the same multiple meaning word.

Name _____   Date _____

Idioms

An **idiom** is a figure of speech. It is an expression that must be "translated" to be understood. An idiom cannot be taken literally.

    Example: Suzanne *goes with the flow.*

        Goes with the flow means that Suzanne is easy to get along with and does not get upset if plans change.

PRACTICE

Read each sentence. What do you think each underlined idiom means? Write your idiom "translation" on the line following the sentence.

    Example: Making this cedar chest was <u>as easy as pie</u>. <u>It was not hard to do.</u>

1. <u>At the eleventh hour</u>, the package arrived. _____

2. It's not nice <u>to bad-mouth</u> one's classmates. _____

3. The teacher <u>was all ears</u> at the sound of whispering voices. _____

4. Winning the tournament was <u>a piece of cake.</u> _____

5. Dad wants to be <u>on the road</u> at 7:00 A.M. _____

6. Anthony is becoming quite the <u>couch potato.</u> _____

    _____

7. Terri is always so <u>wishy-washy</u> when asked to make a decision. _____

    _____

Use each idiom in a sentence.

1. head honcho— _____

2. two peas in a pod— _____

3. a know-it-all— _____

4. at arm's length— _____

Write the meaning for each idiom.

1. At a snail's pace: _____

2. At death's door: _____

WRITE ON!

Choose an idiom from above. On a separate sheet of paper, write a paragraph using the idiom as a starting point.

Name _____   Date _____

Idioms

An **idiom** is a figure of speech. It is an expression that must be "translated" to be understood. An idiom cannot be taken literally.

> Example: Skyler *caught a cold*.
>
> *Caught a cold* means that Skyler is sick.
>
> Skyler cannot actually hold out a net to "catch a cold."

PRACTICE

Write a translation for each italicized idiom on the line following the sentence.

> Example: Sarah filed the papers in the *circular file*.
>
> Meaning: The circular file is a garbage can.

1. Ben and Tilly *don't see eye to eye* on that matter.

   Meaning: _____

2. Bridget completed her project *ahead of time*.

   Meaning: _____

3. Next time you are in town, *drop me a line*.

   Meaning: _____

4. He always walks around with his *head in the clouds*.

   Meaning: _____

5. We have a *fat chance* of passing the chemistry test.

   Meaning: _____

6. She *isn't playing with a full deck* of cards.

   Meaning: _____

7. It takes her *forever and a day* to do anything.

   Meaning: _____

8. You have a *good eye* for decorating.

   Meaning: _____

9. The manager just gave me the same old *song and dance*.

   Meaning: _____

10. Looks like somebody *got up on the wrong side of the bed*.

    Meaning: _____

WRITE ON!

Choose an idiom from above. On a separate sheet of paper, write a paragraph using the idiom as a starting point.

Name _____   Date _____

Idioms

An **idiom** is a figure of speech. It is an expression that must be "translated" to be understood. An idiom cannot be taken literally.

> Example: His elevator doesn't go all the way to the top.
>
> Meaning: He does not think clearly or logically.

PRACTICE

Read each sentence and underline the idiom. Write the meaning of the idiom on the line.

> Example: Terri <u>bends over backwards</u> to please everyone.
>
> Meaning: She tries very hard to make everyone happy.

1. George really likes to lay it on thick.

   Meaning: _____

2. Boy, the Simpsons have really let their house go to the dogs.

   Meaning: _____

3. Mom thinks there is something fishy going on next door.

   Meaning: _____

4. My brother is always getting in my hair!

   Meaning: _____

5. Justin is always shooting off his mouth.

   Meaning: _____

6. The gas station is going to make us pay through the nose for the extra gas.

   Meaning: _____

7. We are going to play it by ear.

   Meaning: _____

8. My sister is all thumbs when it comes to using a hammer and nails.

   Meaning: _____

9. My brother left me high and dry when he met up with his friends.

   Meaning: _____

10. My dad is always selling me short.

    Meaning: _____

WRITE ON!

On a separate sheet of paper, write an essay explaining the idiom, *kick the bucket,* to someone who is not a native speaker of English. Share your explanation with the class.

Name _____   Date _____

Similes

A **simile** is a figure of speech making a comparison using the words *like* or *as* to describe something.
    Example: Vivian's hands are *as cold as ice.*
        As cold as ice describes the noun, hands.

PRACTICE

Underline the simile used in each sentence. Explain its use on the line.

    Example: The tape was <u>as sticky as molasses.</u>   <u>very sticky</u>

1. Max's brain is like a computer. _____

2. Bea can be as stubborn as a mule when she wants something. _____

3. Noah is as thin as a pencil. _____

4. Bryan was as happy as a clam after winning the race. _____

5. Pat is bundled up like a caterpillar in a cocoon. _____

6. Carmen buzzed around like a fly at a picnic. _____

7. Her bedroom looked like a pigsty. _____

Underline the similes in the paragraphs.

    Stephanie was jumping around like a wet hen. Mom asked her what had made her as mad as a hornet. Stephanie said the tire on her bike was as flat as a pancake and she was going to be late for her art class. Mom said, "This will make you as happy as a pig in a poke. Hop in the car and I will have you there in the blink of an eye." "Thanks, Mom! You are like a fairy godmother. You saved the day!"

    This book is as heavy as a concrete block. It is as old as the hills and used to belong to my grandparents. My grandparents used the book to hold up their dining room table. My Dad used to toss the book around as if it were as light as a feather. I will use the book as an anchor for my rowboat.

Write a simile for each topic.

1. book: _____

    _____

2. tennis shoes: _____

    _____

WRITE ON!

On a separate sheet of paper, write a paragraph using at least two similes to describe a favorite food or dessert. Try to make your similes unique. Exchange papers with a classmate. Have the classmate underline the similes used in the paragraph.

Name _____ Date _____

Similes

A **simile** is a figure of speech comparing two things using the words *like* or *as*.

    Example: The truck rumbled like a lion roaring.

        Like a lion roaring describes the sound the truck made.

Underline the simile in each sentence, and write a possible definition on the line next to it.

    Example: Caden was built <u>like a fireplug</u>. <u>Caden was short but sturdy</u>.

1. The Simpsons are as poor as church mice. _____

2. I can read her like a book. _____

3. He was as helpful as a square wheel. _____

4. Talking to him is like talking to a brick wall. _____

5. The water poured from the hole in the wall like a waterfall. _____

6. Teddy looked like he had been through a war and lost. _____

7. The hail looked like golf balls falling from the sky. _____

8. The ice cream was as hard as cement. _____

9. Her chair was like a throne. _____

10. We treated the visiting author like a king. _____

Write your own similes describing the following topics.

1. a best friend:_____

    _____

2. a pet:_____

    _____

3. an assignment: _____

    _____

4. cafeteria food: _____

    _____

On a separate sheet of paper, describe the best (or the worst) food ever served by the cafeteria. Use at least two similes to describe the food, how it tasted, and how it looked.

Name _____   Date _____

Similes

A **simile** is a figure of speech comparing two things using the words *like* or *as*.

  Example: That vitamin water is *like the fountain of youth*.

PRACTICE

Rewrite each sentence using a simile.

1. The dog is big. _____

    _____

2. The old car is unreliable. _____

    _____

3. Phil is grumpy. _____

    _____

4. She is a dancer._____

    _____

5. The pillow is fluffy. _____

    _____

Underline the similes used in the paragraph.

      The telephone was ringing like a three-alarm fire. Barb scurried like a little mouse to answer
the phone before it rang again. On the phone was a fast-talking salesperson trying to sell a vitamin that
promised to make you feel like you were just born. Barb said, "No thanks," and dropped the phone like
a hot potato. Barb went back to waxing the floor until it shone like a newly-minted penny.

Rewrite the paragraph without using any similes.

_____
_____
_____
_____

Which paragraph is more interesting to read? Why?

_____
_____

WRITE ON!

On a separate sheet of paper, write a paragraph describing an ordinary day. Use similes to make the
paragraph more interesting to read.

Name _____   Date _____

Similes

A **simile** is a figure of speech comparing two things using the words *like* or *as*.

    Example: Grandma is *as busy as a bee.*

        Grandma's activity level is being compared to a bee's activity level.

PRACTICE

Write four similes. Underline *like* or *as* in each sentence.

    Example: The baby stretched <u>like</u> a sleepy kitten.

1. _____

    _____

2. _____

    _____

3. _____

    _____

4. _____

    _____

Underline the similes used in the paragraph.

      The sports announcer's voice boomed like a bass drum in a parade as he announced each player's name. When the first player was up at bat, he rattled off the player's statistics like a grocery list. The announcer called each exciting second of the game. During the seventh-inning stretch, he relaxed his vocal chords by neighing like a champion racehorse. Everyone in the ball park laughed upon hearing how horse-like he sounded.

WRITE ON!

On a separate sheet of paper, write an essay using similes to describe an exciting event. Trade papers with a classmate and have him or her underline your similes.

Name _____   Date _____

DAILY Warm-Up 110

Metaphors

A **metaphor** is a figure of speech. A metaphor describes a person, place, or thing in a colorful or interesting way. A metaphor compares two things but does not use the words *like* or *as*.

> Example: That cockroach is *deader than a doornail.*
>
> *Deader than a doornail* describes the condition of the cockroach.

PRACTICE

Interpret the meaning of each italicized metaphor.

> Example: The baby clings *tighter than Velcro* to her mother.
>
> *Tighter than Velcro* means that the baby is holding on tightly to her mother and the mother cannot get free.

1. Shannon is *pricklier than a cactus.*

   Meaning: _____

2. The television reception is *fuzzier than Grandma's old slippers.*

   Meaning: _____

3. He is *prouder than a peacock.*

   Meaning: _____

4. Her ears are *full of potatoes.*

   Meaning: _____

5. Shawn has the *attention span of a flea.*

   Meaning: _____

6. Her eyes were *bigger than saucers.*

   Meaning: _____

7. It is *hotter than a sauna.*

   Meaning: _____

8. Her make-up was *put on with a trowel.*

   Meaning: _____

9. The backyard was a *jungle of plant life.*

   Meaning: _____

10. Her nails were *more dangerous than a grizzly bear's claws.*

    Meaning: _____

WRITE ON!

On a separate sheet of paper, write an essay describing what you do to keep warm on a cold, wintry day. Use metaphors in the paragraph and underline them.

Name _____ Date _____

DAILY
Warm-Up 111

Metaphors

A **metaphor** is a figure of speech. A metaphor describes a person, place, or thing in a colorful or interesting way. A metaphor compares two things but does not use the words *like* or *as*.

> Example: Her legs were *bigger than tree trunks*.
>
> *Bigger than tree trunks* describes the size of her legs.

PRACTICE

Underline each metaphor and write its meaning on the line below.

> Example: Her hair is <u>bigger than a beehive.</u>
>
> Meaning: Her hair is quite tall and blocks people's view.

1. He is stronger than an ox.

   Meaning: _____

2. The brownies were chocolate bricks.

   Meaning: _____

3. She stands straighter than a ruler.

   Meaning: _____

4. The car engine is smoother than a purring cat.

   Meaning: _____

5. Justin's handwriting is worse than a chicken's.

   Meaning: _____

Write your own metaphors for two of the following topics.

> A song: _____
>
> A television program:_____
>
> A train: _____
>
> A superhero:_____
>
> Teeth: _____

WRITE ON!

On a separate sheet of paper, write a paragraph about the president. Use metaphors to describe him. Exchange papers with a classmate. Have the classmate underline the metaphors used in the paragraph.

Name _____   Date _____

Metaphors

A **metaphor** is a figure of speech. A metaphor describes a person, place, or thing in an interesting way. A metaphor compares two things but does not use the words *like* or *as*.

> Example: Tyler *is a walking encyclopedia* of baseball statistics.
>
> *Is a walking encyclopedia* describes that Tyler has a lot of information about baseball.

PRACTICE

Underline the metaphor in each sentence and explain its meaning.

1. That car is an old dinosaur. _____
2. Miss Wilson has a heart of gold. _____
3. Matilda is a lifesaver. _____
4. Chase is a clown when in the classroom._____
5. Sara can add up those numbers faster than an adding machine. _____
6. That story is older than the hills. _____

Rewrite each sentence to include a metaphor.

1. It is an old cat. _____

   _____

2. There is water in the bathtub._____

   _____

3. The bed is messy. _____

   _____

4. The cupboards are neat and tidy. _____

   _____

5. The computer works slowly. _____

   _____

6. The walls are red._____

   _____

7. The birds are singing._____

   _____

WRITE ON!

What does it feel like to ride a skateboard, a swing, or a merry-go-round? On a separate sheet of paper, write a paragraph describing the experience. Use metaphors to help explain your feelings.

Name _____   Date _____

Metaphors

A **metaphor** is a figure of speech, similar to a simile. A metaphor describes a person, place, or thing in a more interesting way. A metaphor compares two things but does not use the words *like* or *as*.

Example of a *metaphor*: Grandma's house is a beehive of activity.

Example of a *simile*: Grandma's busy house is <u>like</u> a beehive.

Meaning: There is a lot going on at Grandma's house.

PRACTICE

Write four metaphors and explain the meaning of each.

Example: Her teeth sparkled brighter than a newly minted penny.

Meaning: Her teeth were very sparkly.

1. _____

Meaning: _____

2. _____

Meaning: _____

3. _____

Meaning: _____

4. _____

Meaning: _____

Read the paragraph. Underline the metaphors. Circle the similes.

Tanya was working like an army ant on her truck. The truck was older than the hills but she loved it. She quickly changed the oil and fixed the brakes. Then, Tanya moved on to the tires. The tires were larger than a tractor's tires and heavier than an elephant. With help from a neighbor, Tanya was able to jack the truck up, remove the old tires, and put on the new tires. Afterwards, Tanya was so tired she almost fell asleep standing up like a horse!

WRITE ON!

On a separate sheet of paper, write about an ordinary household task. Use similes and metaphors to liven up the narrative. Exchange papers with a classmate. Have the classmate underline the metaphors and circle the similes.

Name _____   Date _____

Personification

Personification refers to a figure of speech in which human qualities are given to ideas, things, or animals.

> Examples: The motor *choked and spat* before it died.
>
>   The boulder *refused* to budge.

Underline the personification in each sentence.

1. The sun wrapped me in its warmth.

2. When milk was poured over the cereal, the cereal popped and crackled.

3. The fried chicken was speaking to me, saying, "Eat me!"

4. The newspaper was wrinkled and yellowed with age.

5. The mud clung mightily to his shoes and pants.

6. The cabin welcomed us home after a hard day of hiking.

7. The clay took shape within my hands.

8. The sapling bent and twined gracefully around the trellis.

9. The pencil's sharp point stabbed and poked at the paper.

10. The puppy snuggled and sighed in my arms.

11. The wood glowed with a warm, rosy sheen.

12. The ants attacked the bread and carried it home for their queen.

Use personification to describe two of the items below.

> Example: *leaf*—The leaf danced merrily along the sidewalk.

1. *cat*— _____

2. *star*— _____

3. *tractor*— _____

4. *blanket*— _____

Write a paragraph on a separate sheet of paper. Pick a favorite animal to describe using personification.
Underline the examples of personification.

Name _____   Date _____

Personification

Personification refers to a figure of speech in which human qualities are given to ideas, things, or animals.

> Example: The daisies *were calm* on that windless day.

Underline the sentences in each paragraph where personification is used.

After the long trip, coming home was like hugging an old friend. Marcie tiredly unpacked her suitcases. Some of the clothes were so dirty, they could stand up by themselves. Marcie tossed the dirty clothes into the washing machine. At the twist of the dial, the washer whirred to life, stripping the dirt from the clothes. Marcie then put her suitcases in the attic. The suitcases were lined up as if they were little soldiers waiting for their marching orders. Finally, Marcie was able to lie down on the couch. The couch sighed as it accepted Marcie's weight.

The turtle trudged along. He was barely moving. Finally, the old turtle reached his destination, a patch of sweet grass. The turtle nibbled neatly at the sweet blades of grass until he had his fill. He then slowly ambled to a nearby puddle of fresh water and lapped his fill. When done, the turtle licked his lips as if satisfied with his delightful vegetarian snack. The turtle decided to lie down and rest in the warm sunshine. The sunshine warmed his snug, patterned shell. After a little nap, the rested turtle peeked out of his shell before sticking his head out, stretched his limbs, and began the long journey back to his cozy home.

Use personification to describe each item.

> Example: *door*—The door <u>refused</u> to budge.

1. *elephant*— _____

2. *calculator*— _____

Write a paragraph on a separate sheet of paper. Use personification to describe a favorite item.

Name _____ Date _____

Personification

A figure of speech expresses an idea in a non-literal way. **Personification** is a figure of speech in which an idea, object, or animal is given human characteristics.

    Example: The tree branches *whistled* in the wind.

        Whistled is the human-like quality given to the tree branches.

Finish each sentence using personification.

    Example: The book was interesting.

        The book <u>grabbed the reader's attention</u> from the start.

1. Leslie grew tomatoes _____

2. Her blonde hair _____

3. Bobby's blanket _____

4. The row of trees _____

5. The man changed channels _____

6. The car jolted _____

7. The mangy dog _____

8. The orange tree grew _____

9. The taller buildings _____

10. The old barn _____

Underline the phrases where personification is used.

      The ball flew swiftly towards the hoop and swooshed through the basket. The crowd roared at the three-pointer. The scoreboard came alive with lights flashing and firecrackers shooting from its screen. The basketball court jumped and jiggled under the weight of pounding feet. What a fabulous game!

On a separate sheet of paper, write about an exciting sports event—real or imaginary.
Use personification to describe the event.

Name _____ Date _____

Alliteration

Alliteration is a writing device frequently used in writing poetry to create lines that are pleasing to the ear. When using alliteration, most or all of the words in a sentence begin with the same *sound*. For this reason, alliteration is often used in tongue twisters.

Example: <u>P</u>eter <u>P</u>iper <u>p</u>icked a <u>p</u>eck of <u>p</u>ickled <u>p</u>eppers.

PRACTICE

Use alliteration to describe each animal.

Example: Bear—<u>B</u>umbly, <u>b</u>rown <u>b</u>ear <u>b</u>umped through the <u>b</u>lackberry patch.

1. Cheetah: _____

2. Hippo: _____

3. Kitten: _____

4. Frog:_____

5. Elephant: _____

Practice reading the two alliterative paragraphs below. Read them silently a few times and then take turns reading them aloud to a classmate.

Henrietta Harris

Henrietta Harris is always in a hurry. Henrietta hurries through homework, harmonica practice, and housework. When not hurrying, Henrietta hustles to feed her hamster, Harry. Henrietta also puts fresh hay in Harry's habitat and brushes Harry's hairy hair. Henrietta and Harry are perfect housemates!

Andy Andrews

Andy Andrews anchors the afternoon news. Each afternoon, Andy always angles his armchair towards the camera, adjusts his eyeglasses, and asks, "Are we ready?" Andy Andrews always answers questions from the audience before announcing the afternoon accidents.

WRITE ON!

On a separate sheet of paper, tell about your ideal job using alliteration.

Name _____   Date _____

Onomatopoeia

Onomatopoeia is a writing device often used when writing poetry. Writers use words that have a sound like the *sound* they are trying to convey—like the "*buzzing*" of bees, the "*meows*" of cats, or the "*thump*" of a dog's tail on the floor. Other words that work are *zing*, *zigzag*, *swish*, and *zip*.

Example: The grandfather clock *tick-tocked* quietly in the big living room.

Use onomatopoeia to further describe the words below.

Example: cat <u>meowing and mewling</u>

1. duck _____

2. breaking dish _____

3. sound of a car horn_____

4. applause _____

5. angry dog _____

6. bird_____

7. sleepy cat _____

8. old door opening _____

9. timer going off _____

10. lion _____

11. pig _____

12. racing car _____

WRITE ON!

Write a paragraph on a separate sheet of paper in which you imagine you are a farmer. Describe your day working with the different animals. Use onomatopoeia to suggest the different sounds you hear on the farm.

Name _____ Date _____

Capitalization

Capital letters are used when writing the following words:

- the *first word* in a new sentence
- *proper nouns* (nouns that name specific people, places, or things including the names of months of the year, days of the week, and holidays)
- *titles* of historical events, books, and movies

Think of a specific name for each person, place, or thing listed below.

  Example: movie title: <u>Star Wars</u>

  1. restaurant:_____

  2. park: _____

  3. game: _____

  4. city: _____

  5. state: _____

  6. country: _____

  7. birthday month: _____

  8. best day of the week: _____

  9. favorite holiday: _____

  10. book title: _____

Read the paragraph. Add proofer marks (three lines under the lowercase letter) to indicate where capital letters should be added.

  Example: We always go to the <u>joy</u> <u>luck</u> restaurant for dinner on <u>new</u> <u>year's</u> <u>day</u>.

    On monday we went to the opening of fantastic fast food. fantastic fast food is the latest rage in restaurants. They only serve rapidly prepared food. The food and drinks are all served on paper products, and the customers have to eat standing up. The restaurant is located at the corners of palm avenue and hemlock avenue. If you only have a short time to eat lunch, fantastic fast food is the place to go!

On a separate sheet of paper, write a paragraph describing a special weekend when you went on a trip. Use as many proper nouns as you can when describing your trip. Share the paragraph with a classmate and have him or her underline all the proper nouns.

Name _____   Date _____

Capitalization

Capital letters are used when writing the following words:

- the *first word* in a new sentence
- *proper nouns* (nouns that name specific people, places, or things, including the names of months of the year, days of the week, and holidays)
- *titles* of historical events, books, and movies

Read each paragraph below. Add proofer marks (three lines under the lowercase letter) to indicate where capital letters should be added.

Example: my cat, fido, thinks he is a dog.

Paragraph 1

Every monday, our teacher, mrs. givens, has the class write the weekly homework assignments in our notebooks. Each night, the students are responsible for checking their notebooks and completing the necessary assignments. On friday, all of the assignments are due. Any student not returning his or her homework is given detention the following week.

Paragraph 2

Many schools close for christmas or winter vacation. The vacation starts in mid-december and ends in january. during the vacation, the students and teachers visit with their families, catch up on any chores, or just sleep! What do you like to do on your vacation?

Paragraph 3

Emma is one famous english bulldog! emma has appeared in the spring fling fashion show, been on the front page of the harrisburg press, and been featured on the lbl evening news broadcast. Emma loves all of the attention from the people.

On the back of this page, write a sentence or two using the three rules listed above for using capital letters. Share your sentence(s) with a classmate.

Name _____ Date _____

Commas in a Series

When listing a series of items, use a comma to take the place of the word "and." Use a comma and the word "and" before the final item.

> Example: Marianne has red socks and purple socks and green socks and yellow socks and orange socks.
>
> *Marianne has red socks, purple socks, green socks, yellow socks, and orange socks.*

PRACTICE

Rewrite each sentence using commas to list the series of items.

> Example: When packing for a trip, always remember to pack a toothbrush and toothpaste and hairbrush and shampoo.
>
> When packing for a trip, always remember to pack a toothbrush, toothpaste, hairbrush, and shampoo.

1. Every student needs a pencil box filled with pencils and erasers and markers and rulers and crayons.

   _____

   _____

2. In case of an emergency, every child should know his or her phone number the parents' home and work numbers and home address and emergency meeting place and emergency phone numbers.

   _____

   _____

3. I am wearing a jacket and a scarf and mittens and a hat.

   _____

   _____

4. Many men now go to day spas for special treatments including manicures and pedicures and facials and massages.

   _____

   _____

5. To make a fantastic peanut butter and jelly sandwich, you will need bread and a knife and peanut butter and jelly and a plate.

   _____

   _____

WRITE ON!

Think of a favorite sport or hobby. On the back of this page, make a list of five items needed in order to do the sport or hobby. Rewrite the list in a sentence using commas.

Name _____ Date _____

Commas in Dates

Use **commas** in dates to separate the day of the week from the month.

    Example: Monday, March 31, 2008

Use **commas** in dates to separate the date from the year. Do *not* use a comma when a month and a year are listed without a specific date.

    Examples: March 31, 2008   March 2008

Rewrite each date correctly.

1. Tuesday January 5 2010 _____
2. March 2 2009 _____
3. Friday September 25 2009 _____
4. Wednesday January 27 2010 _____
5. February 14 2008 _____
6. November 30 2009 _____
7. Thursday October 2 2008 _____
8. April 2007 _____
9. Saturday May 24 2008 _____
10. June 21 2009 _____

Add commas where needed in the passages below.

Upcoming School Events

Our school will hold a movie night on Friday April 4 2009. The movie will begin at 6:00 P.M. Everybody is invited to attend. Wear pajamas and bring sleeping bags!

May 9 2009 is the date of the school carnival. The carnival will be held from 4:00 P.M. to 8:00 P.M. There will be plenty of food, drinks, and games. Bring your money and be prepared to have some fun!

Field Day will be on Tuesday June 9, for the primary students, and on Wednesday June 10 for the intermediate students. Wear tennis shoes and shorts and be ready to run around, get wet, and enjoy a cool treat!

The last day of school is Thursday June 11 2009. Enjoy your summer and we will see you again for the start of the new school year in August!

What is happening at your school or in your classroom for the next month? Are there any special events planned? Make a list of dates and events on a separate sheet of paper. If no events are planned at school, look at a calendar and list the dates of five national holidays. Remember to use commas when writing the dates. Have a classmate proofread your work and add commas where needed.

Name _____ Date _____

Commas in Letters

Commas are used in at least three parts of a letter: the date, the salutation or greeting, and the closing. Commas might also be used in the body of the letter.

Examples:

The date: March 22, 2008

Salutation or greeting: Dear Bobby,

Closing: Your friend,

PRACTICE

Proofread the following letters. Add commas where needed for the parts of the letter mentioned above. Don't forget to add the commas in the body of the letter.

Letter #1

June 2 2005

Dear Grandma

   I had a great time visiting you this weekend. It was fun picking berries and making berry pies. It was so funny when the dog ran off with one of the fresh-baked pies! Next time let's make some pumpkin pies.

Love

Brody

Letter #2

December 1 2007

Dear Santa Claus

   I have been a good person this year. I have helped my parents around the house. I took care of my little brother and sister raked leaves kept my room clean and washed the dishes. I have also kept my grades up in school. Since I have been so good this year, I would like to ask you to bring me the latest in video gaming stations and video game cartridges.

Your little helper
Shelley

On a separate sheet of paper, write a letter to a classmate. Underline the commas used in the date, the greeting, and the closure. Check the body of the letter to see if other commas are needed.

Name _____ Date _____

Commas with Conjunctions

Use a **comma** when two sentences (independent clauses) are combined with a conjunction such as *for, and, nor, but,* or, *yet,* or *so.*

    Example: I have a brown house. I have a brown car.

                I have a brown house, and I have a brown car.

PRACTICE

Use a comma and a conjunction to combine each pair of sentences. Try to use different conjunctions in the sentences.

    Example: Marvin did all of his homework last night. He left it at home.

                Marvin did all of his homework last night, but he left it at home.

1. Alaska is the largest state. Alaska has a small population.

    _____

2. The car had a brand new battery. The car would not start.

    _____

3. It was icy cold outside. Inside the home was warm and cozy.

    _____

4. The dogs look fierce and dangerous. The dogs are friendly and lovable.

    _____

5. I brought a cold lunch today. I won't need to use my lunch card.

    _____

6. Jonah's favorite color is red. He also likes blue.

    _____

7. Jenna loves all kinds of frogs. She has decorated her house with frogs.

    _____

8. Paul likes to save all of his change. He keeps the coins separated into different jars.

    _____

9. Mom has an important business meeting today. She wore her "power suit."

    _____

10. The 6th grade students are wearing hats with tassels. They are graduating today.

    _____

WRITE ON!

Write four pairs of sentences on the back of this page. Exchange papers with a classmate. Have the classmate rewrite the sentences using a comma and a conjunction to combine each pair.

Apostrophes for Possessives

Use an **apostrophe** + s (*'s*) to show ownership.

> Example: That dress was a favorite of my older sister.
>
> The dress was once my older *sister's* favorite.

Rewrite each sentence to show ownership.

> Example: John has the sharpest skates on the rink.
>
> <u>John's skates are the sharpest on the rink.</u>

1. Chaz has a black horse named Blackie.

   _____

2. Michelle has the messiest desk in the school!

   _____

3. Brent has a film in the Valley Film Festival.

   _____

4. Our newspaper boy has a Super Speedy bike in red.

   _____

5. Alex has a fake fur coat.

   _____

6. In the fashion show, Jean wore a pink dress.

   _____

7. The bow fell off of the stuffed teddy bear.

   _____

8. The gavel belongs on the desk of the judge.

   _____

9. Grandma has a beach house overlooking the ocean.

   _____

10. The red and gold luggage belongs to Max.

    _____

Write four sentences using possessives on the back of this page. Underline the words that show ownership with the apostrophe + s (*'s*).

Name _____ Date _____

Apostrophes for Possessives

Use an **apostrophe** + *s* (*'s*) to show ownership.

Example: The house belongs to John.

It is *John's* house.

Underline the sentences that can be rewritten in possessive form.

    This weekend we went to the house of my friend. Bob lives in the green house, about three houses down the street. We went to help Bob build a clubhouse. Our first step was borrowing tools from the dad and uncle of Bob. Then we started laying the boards to build the floor of the clubhouse. Next, we attached the sides to the clubhouse. Finally, we were able to put the roof on. Jenna, the sister of Bob, came out of the house when we were done. She wanted to play in the clubhouse. We told her no way! She began to cry so we gave her a "special membership" and let her into the clubhouse.

Rewrite the underlined sentences using possessive forms.

1. _____

   _____

2. _____

   _____

3. _____

   _____

4. _____

   _____

If you could be on a game show, which one would you be on? Why? Write your response on a separate sheet of paper. Use possessives in the paragraph and underline them.

Name _____   Date _____

Apostrophes for Plural Possessives

A **possessive** shows ownership.

To make a plural noun ending in "**s**" possessive, add an apostrophe after the "**s**'" to show possession.

    Example: The *girls'* team has won the championship!

To make a plural noun not ending in "**s**" possessive, add an apostrophe and an "**'s**."

    Example: The *children's* playground will be dedicated today.

Rewrite each sentence using a plural possessive noun.

    Example: The dogs have kennels in the backyard.

               The dogs' kennels are in the backyard.

1. The hospital for children is located in Madera.

   _____

2. The restroom for men is on the right.

   _____

3. The instrument cases for the band members are on the bus.

   _____

4. The blankets were made by the society of women.

   _____

5. The brushes of the painters were cleaned.

   _____

6. The ducks dropped their feathers on the ground.

   _____

7. The donations from the people were greatly needed.

   _____

8. The jackets of the boys were on the floor.

   _____

9. The singing of the birds is beautiful.

   _____

On a separate sheet of paper, write about a school activity such as a play, concert, or a classroom performance. Use at least three plural possessives in the story and underline them.

Name _____   Date _____

Apostrophes for Shared Possession

To indicate ownership between more than one person, it is important to recognize what is owned and by whom.

When *two people own the same item,* only the second person shows ownership.

    Example: We are going to my grandma and grandpa's house.

When *two people own different items,* both names show ownership.

    Example: Wendy's and Joanie's houses are on this street.

Rewrite each sentence to show either joint ownership of the same item or individual ownership of different items.

    Example: The excuses of Gabriel and Marcus are not believable.

                Gabriel's and Marcus's excuses are not believable.

1. The fluffy dog belongs to Martha and George.

    _____

2. The saddle is for the horse of my aunt and my uncle.

    _____

3. The bathrooms in the houses and condos have been updated.

    _____

4. The engines on the helicopters and airplanes have been replaced.

    _____

5. Billy and Willy dropped the cell phones on the ground.

    _____

6. The new contract is for the operators and mechanics.

    _____

7. The large lounge is for the employees and visitors.

    _____

8. The audition for the boys and girls is today.

    _____

9. The bikes of the first graders and the second graders were locked up.

    _____

On a separate sheet of paper write about something you share (or own) with a sibling or family member. Underline the possessive words.

Apostrophes for Words Ending in "s"

A possessive shows ownership and in most cases, an "**s**" and an apostrophe are added to the word to indicate possession. What do you do when the word already ends in the letter "**s**"?

Singular Words

For singular words that end in *s*, add an apostrophe and *s*.

> Example: Today is the *boss's* birthday.

For singular words that do not end in *s*, add an apostrophe and *s*.

> Example: Today is *Secretary's* Day.

Plural Words

For plural words that end in *s*, add an apostrophe.

> Example: The *cats'* collars are brand new.

For plural words that do not end in *s*, add an apostrophe and *s*.

> Example: The *oxen's* harnesses need to be adjusted.

Does the underlined word name one noun or more than one noun? Write singular or plural on the line.

> Example: The <u>dress's</u> hem is coming undone. <u>singular</u>

1. The <u>doctor's</u> advice should be taken. _____

2. The <u>dresses'</u> colors are too bright. _____

3. The <u>boss's</u> decision was followed. _____

4. <u>Chris's</u> turtle is always digging holes. _____

5. The math <u>classes'</u> teachers are always on time. _____

6. The juice <u>glasses'</u> design was custom made. _____

7. The <u>ladies'</u> restroom is sparkling clean. _____

8. The <u>children's</u> library is open today. _____

9. The <u>movie's</u> ending was a surprise. _____

10. The <u>elephants'</u> noses are huge. _____

Rewrite each phrase to show ownership.

> Example: the toys of the sisters <u>the sisters' toys</u>

1. the wallet belonging to Luis_____

2. the bones are from the bass _____

On the back of this page write three rules that will help you know if a word showing ownership is singular or plural.

Name _____ Date _____

Apostrophes in Contractions

An **apostrophe** is used when writing a contraction. A **contraction** combines two words to create one shorter word. The apostrophe takes the place of the deleted letters.

Examples: would + not = *wouldn't* (the letter *o* has been replaced with an apostrophe)
can + not = *can't* (the letters *n* and *o* have been replaced with an apostrophe)
she + would = *she'd* (the letters *woul* have been replaced with an apostrophe)

PRACTICE

Write the contraction for each pair of words.

1. let us _____
2. they are _____
3. you are _____
4. could not _____
5. they will _____
6. I have _____
7. we will _____
8. he is _____

9. will not _____
10. would not _____
11. must not _____
12. did not _____
13. is not _____
14. can not _____
15. she had _____
16. you would _____

Read the paragraphs. Underline the pairs of words that can be written as contractions. Write the contractions above the words.

On the first day of camp, the camp director gave his world famous speech. "I am Mr. Grieg. You will call me Mr. Grieg. I have been the camp director for more than 50 years. Is there anybody here who has been coming to this camp for as long as I have? I did not think so. You are here at camp for many reasons. Some of you did not come by choice.

"This is Mrs. Grieg. You will call her Mrs. Grieg. She is the camp cook and the camp activities director. When I am napping, she will be in charge of everything here. This is my son, Griffin Grieg. You may call him Mr. Griffin. He is third-in-command. He will make sure that you are in bed at 8:00 PM every night and up at 6:00 AM every morning. If you have any questions, ask Mr. Griffin. Thank you."

WRITE ON!

On a separate sheet of paper, discuss whether or not you would like to go to Mr. Grieg's camp. Reread the paragraph. Can you add any contractions?

Name _____ Date _____

Apostrophes in Contractions

An **apostrophe** is used when writing a contraction. A **contraction** combines two words to create one shorter word. The apostrophe takes the place of the deleted letters.

Examples: were + not = *weren't* (the letter *o* has been replaced with an apostrophe)

let + us = *let's* (the letter *u* has been replaced with an apostrophe)

you + have = *you've* (the letters *ha* have been replaced with an apostrophe)

Write the two words that make each contraction.

Example: doesn't   <u>does</u> + <u>not</u>

1. you'd _____ + _____   10. shouldn't _____ + _____
2. might've _____ + _____   11. won't _____ + _____
3. they'd _____ + _____   12. we'd _____ + _____
4. hadn't _____ + _____   13. who's _____ + _____
5. we've _____ + _____   14. mustn't _____ + _____
6. they've _____ + _____   15. hasn't _____ + _____
7. she'll _____ + _____   16. he'll _____ + _____
8. weren't _____ + _____   17. I'm _____ + _____
9. don't _____ + _____   18. they'll _____ + _____

Rewrite the underlined words in each sentence to form a contraction.

Example: I <u>would not</u> have been late, but I missed the bus. <u>wouldn't</u>

1. Kenny <u>could not</u> get off the bus. _____
2. The bus <u>will not</u> be late today. _____
3. <u>Who is</u> bringing the dessert to the party? _____
4. <u>Do not</u> antagonize your little brother! _____
5. <u>I will</u> be in big trouble if I lose the house key again! _____
6. He <u>had not</u> lost his homework after all. _____
7. That answer <u>does not</u> make sense. _____
8. <u>They are</u> always going on a trip to somewhere unusual. _____

On a separate sheet of paper, write four sentences with contractions but leave out the apostrophes. Exchange papers with a classmate. Have the classmate read the sentences and add the missing apostrophes.

Name _____ Date _____

Hyphens

A **hyphen** (-) is used in the following situations:

To join two words serving as a single adjective

    Example: one-way street

To write compound numbers

    Example: forty-three

To avoid confusion or an awkward combination of letters

    Examples: shell-like not shelllike

Add hyphens where needed in each phrase.

1. ice cream cone
2. twenty three dollars
3. well known author
4. high wire act
5. toll free number
6. thirty nine years old

Underline the pairs of words that need a hyphen. Write the words correctly above.

    I am Max Axelrod, a world renowned journalist. I can make even the most boring story interesting to read. Right now, I am searching for Fleet Johnson. Fleet Johnson was the world's fastest runner. During the 1930s, everyone knew who Fleet was, but today, nobody does. Now, Fleet Johnson would be ninety nine years old. I am driving along a winding, rut filled road. On one side of my car are mountains rising higher than the eye can see. On the other side of my car are cliffs that drop directly onto sharp rocks that can tear a person apart. I am looking for a lighthouse. I heard, through my super secret sources, that Fleet Johnson was spending her retirement years making sure ships did not crash into the treacherous coastline. Aha, I spy the lighthouse up ahead! I quickly park my car as close to the lighthouse as possible. I gather up all of my equipment and lock the car. I knock on the old, wind weathered door. The door slowly creaks open. A wrinkled face with twinkling blue eyes peeks out. "Well, hello Max!" "Hi, Great Grandma! I am here for the weekend!"

On the back of this page make a list of other words that need hyphens. List at least four. Compare your list to a classmate's list. Add words from each other's lists to your own to learn more hyphenated words.

Name _____ Date _____

Hyphens

A **hyphen** (-) is used in the following situations:

With certain prefixes (ex- meaning former, self- meaning all) and suffixes (-elect)

    Example: ex-mayor, self-starter, governor-elect

Between a capitalized letter and a word

    Examples: T-shirt; X-ray

With dates, figures, or letters

    Examples: mid-1970s; twenty-two; U-turn

To break a word (between syllables) at the end of a line. The exception to this rule is that one never divides a one-syllable word. If a one-syllable word doesn't fit at the end of the line, move the whole word to the following line.

    Example: independent—in-de-pend-ent could be separated in any of the spaces between syllables indicated with hyphens.

PRACTICE

Underline the words in each sentence that require a hyphen. Rewrite the word with a hyphen on the line following the sentence.

1. The expert knows everything about midcentury art. _____

2. The club sells Tshirts for $9.50 at all home games. _____

3. The exfootball star is signing autographs at the mall today. _____

4. The mayorelect is holding an election party tomorrow night. _____

5. Maria is so selfabsorbed! _____

6. Axel is the exdrummer for Fast Beat. _____

7. My little sister plays on the local Tball team. _____

Use hyphens to divide each word into syllables. Use a dictionary if necessary.

1. calcify _____

2. bulletin _____

3. sapling _____

4. thermometer _____

5. crystallize _____

6. subsequent _____

7. untouchable _____

8. whirlpool _____

9. emollient _____

10. croquet _____

WRITE ON!

On a separate sheet of paper, write five sentences. In each sentence include a word that needs a hyphen. Exchange papers with a classmate. Have the classmate add the missing hyphen to each sentence. Check each other's work.

Name _____   Date _____

DAILY
Warm-Up 134

Colons

A **colon** (:) is used after a formal greeting in a letter.

    Example: Dear Editor:

A **comma** (,) is used after a personal (informal) greeting in a letter.

    Example: Dear Grandma,

PRACTICE

Determine if the greetings below are for formal or personal greetings. Place a colon after formal greetings and a comma after personal greetings. Write the words *formal* or *personal* after your choice.

    Examples: Dear Mom, <u>personal</u>

               Dear Mr. Wilson: <u>formal</u>

1. To Whom It May Concern _____

2. Dear Sir or Madam _____

3. Hi Seth _____

4. Dear Principal Henry _____

5. Hey Beth _____

6. Dear Uncle Bill and Aunt Lorna _____

7. Hi Sis _____

8. Dear President _____

9. Dear Alonzo and Jackie _____

10. Dear Auntie Kathie _____

Write two more personal greetings and two more formal greetings. Use the correct punctuation mark after each greeting.

    Personal

    1. _____

    2. _____

    Formal

    1. _____

    2. _____

WRITE ON!

On a separate sheet of paper, write a short letter to a business to compliment or complain about a product. Remember to use a colon after the greeting.

Name _____ Date _____

Colons

A **colon** (:) is used in a variety of ways including the following situations:

- After a greeting in a business letter

> Example: Dear Principal Hughes:

- To separate a book's title from its subtitle

> Example: *Getting Ahead: 10 Ways to Be a Success*

PRACTICE

Underline the greetings that need to be followed by a colon. Add a colon to those greetings and a comma to less formal ones.

1. Dear Sir or Madam
2. Dear Mom and Dad
3. Hello Dear Friend
4. Hi Grandma and Grandpa
5. To Whom It May Concern

6. Dear President Thomas
7. Customer Service
8. Dear Aunt Cecilia
9. Hi Sis
10. Dear Principal Smith

Use a colon to separate the main title from its subtitle.

> Example: *Bulldogs: How to Train Them So That They Don't Train You!*

1. *Surf Like a Pro Ten Easy Steps to Mastering the Basics*
2. *The Electoral College So Confusing Nobody Can Explain It*
3. *What's Up With That? 15 Mysteries Easily Explained*
4. *Iggy The Man Behind the Name*
5. *Woolly Mammoth and Man Did They Ever Walk the Earth Together?*
6. *Carbonation The Real Pop Behind Soda Pop*
7. *Using Your Digital Camera How to Take Pictures Like a Pro*
8. *Bottlee Water versus Tap Water The Real Truth*
9. *Hybrids Two Kinds of Cars Rolled Into One*
10. *Cats Feline or Fiendish?*

WRITE ON!

On a separate sheet of paper, write five book titles with subtitles. Remember to use a colon to separate the main title from the subtitle.

Name _____ Date _____

Colons

A **colon** (:) can be used to introduce a series of items after an independent clause. (An independent clause is a complete sentence by itself.)

Example: We packed many camping items: sleeping bags, tents, backpacks, and hiking boots.

Rewrite each sentence using an independent clause and a colon.

Example: Some of the programs on television are mysteries, comedies, and musicals.
There are different programs on television: mysteries, comedies, and musicals.

1. The school's colors are red, black, and white.

    _____

2. Mom went to the bank, then to the drycleaners, and finally to the grocery store.

    _____

3. Elijah, Jalen, Anthony, and Enrique are on the football team.

    _____

4. The recipe required kiwi, mangoes, cucumbers, and carrots.

    _____

5. The students need to wear a shirt, pants or skirt, and sneakers as part of their school uniform.

    _____

6. The booster club sold popcorn, hot dogs, soda, and candy bars during the game.

    _____

7. Preston has ten pencils, eight crayons, three markers, and twenty rulers in his desk.

    _____

8. Marta has been to Australia, Europe, and Africa.

    _____

On the back of this page write three independent clauses followed by lists of items. Remember to use colons to separate the independent clauses from the items listed in each sentence.

Name _____ Date _____

Colons

Use a **colon** (:) after *as follows, the following*, and other similar expressions. (A colon does not follow variations of the verb "to be".)

> Example: To embroider a piece of fabric, do the following three things: place the fabric inside the embroidery hoop, thread the needle, and push the needle up from below the fabric and then back down.

Rewrite the sentences by adding colons, commas, and end punctuation to the sentences below. Circle the sentences where a colon was needed.

> Examples: Follow these three steps: get up, get dressed, and go to school.
>
> Every morning I get up, get dressed, and go to school.

1. The job requires the following attributes good speaking skills great people skills and hard work

   _____

2. Pack the following items hiking boots shorts sunscreen and a hat

   _____

3. Michelle read a book wrote a story and painted a picture

   _____

4. This is what happened the boys hit a ball the ball broke the window the homeowner was not happy

   _____

5. Roscoe ate the pizza cookies hot dogs and potato chips

   _____

6. In case of an emergency, follow the following steps get to a safe place call 9-1-1 stay calm

   _____

7. Tanya reported that the recycling drive raised one hundred dollars and the coat drive provided fifty coats

   _____

On a separate sheet of paper, write a paragraph explaining three different ways to use a colon.

Name _____ Date _____

Quotation Marks

Quotation marks (" ") are used to show a person's exact words. Commas and periods are always placed within the quotation marks. Question marks and exclamation marks are placed inside the quotation marks if their purpose is to punctuate the quotation.

Example: Sarah said, "I'm going on a family vacation."

Quotation marks are not used when it is a statement and not a person's exact words.

Example: Sarah said she is going on a family vacation.

Read the sentences. Place quotation marks around the speakers' exact words. Cross out sentences that do not need quotation marks.

Example: "Mom! I can't find my shoes!" yelled Joseph.

1. Down! said Dad to the dog.

2. Marla, said Mrs. Harrison, Do you need help?

3. Go to school! said Dad.

4. The children placed their work in the basket.

5. The weatherperson reported that there would be showers on Wednesday.

6. The children were scared and screaming when the jack-in-the-box popped up during class.

7. The classmates yelled, Happy Birthday!

8. The police officer asked the drivers to avoid the traffic accident.

9. Have you ever read, *Why Did the Chicken Cross the Road?* asked the professor.

10. Shhh, the baby is sleeping, whispered Grandma.

11. Scott yelled, Yeah Chargers! when his team scored some points.

12. Dad is always telling us to clean up our rooms.

13. The principal said, Good job, the campus looks very clean.

14. The coach asked, Are there any questions?

15. Who made all of these beautiful cards? asked the principal.

On the back of this page, write three sentences that show someone's exact words. Remember to use quotation marks to show what the person said.

Name _____   Date _____

Quotation Marks

Quotation marks (" ") are used to show a person's exact words. Commas and periods are placed within the quotation marks.

     Example: Dan said, "I practice the piano every day after school."

When writing dialogue, start a new paragraph whenever a different person speaks.

     Example: Dan said, "I have been playing the piano for ten years."

          "Me, too," said Amy. "I take lessons from Mrs. Howard on Elm Street."

          "I go to Mrs. Guerney on Hope Street. My sister used to take lessons from her, too.

          When I grow up, I want to be a concert pianist!"

Rewrite the paragraph on a separate sheet of paper to show what each person said.

Guess what! yelled Mavis. What? asked Dewey. I finally made it onto the Principal's List!

Wow! That's great, Mavis! Thanks, Dewey. I worked so hard this quarter. I can't believe I made

straight A's in all my classes. You know how hard spelling is for me. But I studied hard for every

week's spelling test. Good for you, Mavis. I made Honor Roll. I had all As and Bs. That's great,

Dewey! You did a good job, too! said Mavis. Let's go and get a root beer to celebrate! suggested

Dewey. Thanks, Dewey. You're a great friend! Let's go get that root beer, said Mavis.

On a separate sheet of paper, write a dialogue between you and a friend, a parent, or a sibling.
Remember to use quotation marks to show the exact words of each person.

Name _____ Date _____

Quotation Marks

Quotation marks (" ") are used when writing the titles of minor works including songs, short stories, essays, short poems, and one-act plays.

    Example: The choir sang "My Country 'Tis of Thee" at the celebration.

Quotation marks (" ") are also used when writing parts of a whole, such as chapters in a book, articles from a newspaper, magazine, or journal, TV episodes, or radio series.

    Example: My family used to listen to "The Lone Ranger" on the radio.

Write a title for each topic. Remember to use quotation marks.

1. Song title: _____

2. Short story: _____

3. Poem: _____

4. Book chapter: _____

5. TV episode: _____

6. Radio series: _____

7. Essay: _____

8. Article: _____

Read the paragraph. Add quotation marks to any titles.

    Tonight is the final episode of Can They Spell It! I have been waiting to see this finale for weeks. I can't wait to see if Cash or Chase wins in the showdown. They are both very good. After the show, I will turn on my radio and listen to the recap on What Happened After the Show? This program, hosted by R U Listening, has interviews with the contestants and gives a sneak peek as to what happened behind the scenes. Then, next week, I will read even more about the show in a column called Spell Watch in the weekly TV Guide issue. In my current affairs class, I even wrote an essay, Cash and Chase: the Showdown. My teacher guessed I loved the show!

On a separate sheet of paper, write an essay about some of your favorites. Briefly explain why you like a specific book, TV show, and movie. Punctuate the titles carefully.

Indenting Paragraphs

Indenting means starting the first word of each new paragraph a few spaces to the right. Indenting a paragraph makes it easier for the reader to know that new information is being presented. It also makes it easier for the reader to go back to find a specific piece of information.

Example:

> The rocket ship had lost all power. It was spinning out of control in space. The astronauts were unable to control the ship's movements. If power was not restored soon, the astronauts were doomed to a life of spinning crazily around in outer space.

PRACTICE

Read the sentences below. Mark paragraphs using the paragraph (¶) editing mark. Add other punctuation as needed on the lines provided.

Have you ever wondered what it would be like to be the tallest or the

shortest person in the world_____ You might think it would be great

to be the tallest because you would be able to see over everyone else.

You might end up being a great basketball player. But think of the

downside of being the tallest person in the world. You would have a

hard time finding shoes that would fit. People would stare and point

at you and would probably ask you, _____How is the weather up

there_____ _____ You might also have health problems from always

having to bend and sit awkwardly in order to fit into furniture and

cars that were too small for you. What about being the smallest person in the world_____ You could be

a spy disguised as a child or, even better, pay child prices when going to the movies! But you might not

be taken seriously because you would be so small. They might think you were "cute" and always try to

pick you up. They might call you "Shorty," or they might think you were a kid when you went to apply

for a job.

WRITE ON!

Which would you rather be, eight feet tall or two feet tall? Why? On a separate sheet of paper, write three paragraphs to answer the question. Be sure to indent the paragraphs.

Paragraph Titles

The **title** is always underlined or typed in italic print and written in the middle of the first line of the page. The title should give the reader an idea of what will be covered in the paragraph. When writing the title, the important words (usually words with three or more letters) are always capitalized.

Example: <u>The Red-Eyed Tree Frog</u> or *The Red-Eyed Tree Frog*

Read each paragraph. Write an appropriate title on the line above it.

Paragraph 1

_____

I hate mornings! It always seems just as I am in the middle of a nice, deep, cozy sleep, that nasty alarm clock goes off! I always groan when I hear it and beg for just 15 minutes more of sleep. But, I know I have to get up and I do. I just wish mornings could start at around 10:00 A.M.!

Paragraph 2

_____

Gloria is always missing school. She has one excuse after another. Unfortunately, each excuse is just as lame as the previous excuse. Can you believe she missed school for three weeks because she was having a "brain transplant"? That's what she said!

Paragraph 3

_____

Benicia is a water town located in the Bay Area. The land of Benicia was bought by Rogert Semple and Thomas Larkin for $100. They bought the land from Spain's last Commandant General, General Mariano C. Vallejo. The town was named after General Vallejo's wife, Dona Francisca Benicia Carillo de Vallejo.

Paragraph 4

_____

Doing the laundry is easy. First separate your laundry into different piles: lights, darks, and towels. Then wash each pile of laundry together. As each load finishes in the washing machine, put it in the dryer and then start the next load in the washing machine. Finally, when the dryer dings, take the clothes out and fold them immediately to prevent wrinkles.

On a separate sheet of paper, write a paragraph on a topic of your choice. Exchange papers with a classmate. Have the classmate add an appropriate title to the paragraph.

Name _____   Date _____

Paragraph Margins

Margins are the white space (border) around all four sides of the page. Many margins are one inch (1"). This means there is 1" of space on each of the four sides. The writing (or text) fits within the given space. Margins serve a variety of purposes:

- Margins can make the paper more visually appealing to the reader.
- Margins can make it easier to read, giving the eye a rest at the end of a line.
- Margins give the reader space to make notes or jot questions or comments about what has just been read.

PRACTICE

Using a ruler, check the measurements of the margins for a textbook.

Textbook _____

Left Margin: _____   Right Margin: _____

Top Margin: _____   Bottom Margin: _____

Rewrite the text below in paragraph form. Indent the first word. The rest of the text should go from margin to margin.

Everyday after school, I take my dog, Pepper, for a walk.

We always take the same route. We head down

the street and to the park. We play in the park for a while.

Pepper loves to go down the kiddie slide.

Then we stop for a drink of water and

head back home.

Walking Pepper is a nice way to unwind after a day at school.

_____

_____

_____

_____

_____

WRITE ON!

Use a separate sheet of paper to write a paragraph explaining why it is a good idea to use margins.

Name _____ Date _____

Proofreading

Proofreading is a method of checking a writing selection for errors in capitalization, spelling, grammar, or punctuation. Use the following proofreading marks to mark errors:

Proofreading Marks	
Add comma $\wedge$	Insert word $\wedge$
Add period $\odot$	Misspelled sp
Capitalize <u>b</u>	New paragraph ¶
Delete ~~the dog~~	Lower case ℓc

Use the proofreading marks to correct each sentence.

Example: always wash ~~your~~ hands after us~~e~~ing the restroom.

1. bob and sue like to eat at Ho ming's Restaurant.

2. where is Benicia.

3. The new television seeson is starting soon.

4. Where Barbara?

5. R the glasses in the dishwasher clean or dity

6. the ribbons aer four the birthday presents.

7. Mom bought four new tires for in bloom the antique vehicle.

8. A ruler iz helpful when measuring small items

9. The map shows the different routes we can take to get to seattle washington.

10. Mrs. tomlinson taught me to make delicious homemade bread pies and a cake!

Use a pencil and a separate sheet of paper. Write four sentences with errors and missing punctuation. Exchange papers with a classmate. Have the classmate use the proofreader's marks to correct each sentence.

Name _____   Date _____

Proofreading

Proofreading is a method of checking a writing selection for errors in capitalization, spelling, grammar, or punctuation. Use the following proofreading marks to mark errors:

Proofreading Marks

Add comma ⋏	Insert word ^
Add period ⊙	Misspelled sp
Capitalize <u>b</u>	New paragraph ¶
Delete ~~the dog~~ ℮	Lower case ⱡ ^{lc}

Use the proofreading marks to correct the errors in each sentence.

  Example: <u>h</u>e always suffers from Extreme "bedhead."

1. we like taking our dogs to the local dog park

2. horatio bought a knew brand of peanut butter

3. what do you think of the name franklin for my new turtle?

4. how many grains of san are one teaspoon?

5. Frank and mike give people parking tickets

Use proofreading marks to correct the paragraph.

did you no that you can buy nsurnc for your pet? That's right! Since pets aer living longer and being treated mor like family members than animals, many companies are now offering insurance to help your pet live long and full life Depending upon the breed of your pet, the kost of the insurance can be cheap or expensive. Before you jump on the insurance bandwagon, check into the costs and see if it would benefit your pet and your budget.

On a separate sheet of paper, write a paragraph about your pet, or a pet you wish you had. Trade it with a classmate when you are done. Proofread each others' work using the proofreader marks above. If you find other errors, underline them and write the correction in the margin of the paper.

Proofreading

Proofreading is a method of checking a writing selection for errors in capitalization, spelling, grammar, or punctuation. Use the following proofreading marks to mark errors:

Proofreading Marks	
Add comma ⋏	Insert word ^
Add period ⊙	Misspelled sp
Capitalize <u>b</u>	New paragraph ¶
Delete ~~the dog~~ ℓ	Lower case ⌿ lc

PRACTICE

Use proofreading marks to correct the errors in each paragraph.

Parking meters

Whenevr a driver travels to a big city, the driver might see parking meters. The city place parking meters on city streets to generate revenue. hen a driver parks on by a parking meter, the driver places coins in the parking meter The parking meter gives a certain amount of time based upon the amount of money fed into the parking meter. Once the time is upp, the driver needs to move the car or risk getting a parking ticket.

Dog Rescue

Have you ever thought you kould save a dog's life? You kan! Instead of buying a puppy, why not visit a local animal shelter At the animal shelter you will see all kinds of dogs—big ones, little ones, furry ones, funny ones—a dog to fit any kind ov family or lifestyle. by adopting a dog from a shelter, you are not only saving the dog's life you are also getting a new best friend.

Have you ever been to an animal shelter? Write about the experience. If you have not been to an animal shelter, interview someone who has gone to one. Write about the experience, the animals, and the care they were given. Trade papers with a classmate and proof each others' work.

Name _____   Date _____

Proofreading

Proofreading is a method of checking a piece of writing for any errors in capitalization, spelling, grammar, or punctuation.

+--+
| **Proofreading Marks** |
| |
| Add comma ⋏   Insert word ^ |
| Add period ⊙   Misspelled sp |
| Capitalize b̲   New paragraph ¶ |
| Delete ~~the dog~~ ℓ   Lower case 𝒫 ˡᶜ |
+--+

PRACTICE

Use the proofreading marks to correct the following paragraph.

　　　Every wednesday night our troop hosts bowling night the local bowling alley. kids from all over the city can bowl for free, if they bring a can of soup or a gently used toy to donate to a needy child The kids are put into teams by ability not by age, and then the games begin. For the beginning bowlers, there is bumper bowling. In bumper bowling, inner tubes are put in the gutters. This makes it easier for the beginner bowler to roll the bowling ball down the middle of the lane and not throw "gutter balls" for the intermediate and advanced bowlers, regular lanes aer used. After everyone has bowled to games, snacks are provided by the bowling alley. All of the bowlers get a hot dog, chips, and a soda. To earn extra money, the troops sell homemade desserts like brownies and cookies. The bowlers get to sit around and visit and make new friends while they eat. It's a great way to learn a sport, meet knew people, and help the community out at the same time!

WRITE ON!

Use a pencil. On the lines below, write about something you have done to help the community, a neighbor, or a friend. Make errors in capitalization, spelling, grammar, and punctuation. Exchange papers with a classmate. Have the classmate use proofreading marks to correct the sentences.

_____

_____

_____

_____

_____

Name _____ Date _____

Dictionary Skills: Alphabetical Order

To know how to use a dictionary effectively and efficiently, one must know how to put words in **alphabetical order**.

Example: eagle   **Alphabetical Order:** ant
                ant   bear
                dog   cat
                bear   dog
                cat   eagle

Rewrite each list of words in alphabetical order.

List 1   **List 2**

space   _____   refrigerator   _____

alien   _____   stove   _____

astronaut   _____   sink   _____

travel   _____   oven   _____

pack   _____   microwave   _____

stars   _____   blender   _____

food   _____   toaster   _____

identification   _____   dishwasher   _____

mechanical   _____   faucet   _____

repair   _____   convection   _____

WRITE ON!

Besides alphabetical order, how else could words be organized? Which way is the most efficient? Why? Write your response on a separate sheet of paper.

Name _____ Date _____

DAILY
Warm-Up 149

Dictionary Skills: Guide Words

Each page of a dictionary has a pair of guide words. **Guide words** are at the top of each page. The guide words are in alphabetical order. Guide words tell the first and last entry words found on that particular dictionary page.

PRACTICE

Pair up the guide words so that they are in alphabetical order. The first one has been done for you.

bed	web	family	belonging	slanted	premiere
pillow	drain	rested	breakfast	~~backyard~~	mainstream
frock	window	slept	stove	lattice	cement
fence	sofa	morning	tea	~~arboreal~~	settling

1. arboreal—backyard _____   7. _____

2. _____   8. _____

3. _____   9. _____

4. _____   10. _____

5. _____   11. _____

6. _____   12. _____

Using a dictionary, write the guide words for the following entry words.

1. cement: _____ _____

2. mainstream: _____ _____

3. family: _____ _____

4. breakfast: _____ _____

5. sofa: _____ _____

6. fence: _____ _____

WRITE ON!

On a separate sheet of paper, write two or three sentences explaining the importance of guide words in a dictionary.

Name _____ Date _____

Dictionary Skills: Entry Words

An **entry word** is a main word listed in the dictionary. Each entry word is in alphabetical order and is usually shown in bold print.

For each entry word, a dictionary will show the following:

- the part of speech
- how to pronounce the word
- the definition of the word
- how to use the word

- any derivations of the word
- possibly a picture of the word
- sample sentence using the word

PRACTICE

Look up each word in a dictionary. If the entry word includes the item in the top column, place a check mark (✓) in the box.

Words	Part of Speech	Pronunciation	Definition	Usage	Derivations	Pictures	Examples of Use
1. Brilliance							
2. Embellish							
3. Perfection							
4. Announcement							
5. Creation							
6. Luncheon							
7. Luxuries							
8. Impoverish							
9. Bandage							
10. Fragile							

WRITE ON!

On a separate sheet of paper, write a paragraph using as many of the words above as you can. Share the paragraph with a classmate.

Name _____   Date _____

Dictionary Skills: Definitions

A dictionary provides a definition (or definitions) for each entry word. A **definition** tells the meaning of the word.

PRACTICE

Use a dictionary to find a definition for each word.

   Example: hysteria—to over-react to a given situation

1. guerilla: _____

2. esteem: _____

3. novelty:_____

4. valance: _____

5. potable:_____

6. competition: _____

7. wrangle: _____

8. zealot:_____

9. abate: _____

10. Xerox: _____

11. bellicose: _____

12. awkward: _____

13. cinema:_____

14. suture:_____

15. chicanery:_____

WRITE ON!

Which word and definition surprised you? Why? Write a short explanation on the lines below.

_____

_____

_____

_____

Name _____   Date _____

DAILY Warm-Up 152

Dictionary Skills: Multiple Meanings

Some words can be used as nouns or as verbs. They sound the same,
but have **multiple meanings**.

Example: I went to the *dance*. (Dance is a *noun*.)

I *dance* well. (Dance is a *verb*.)

PRACTICE

Write the meanings for each word as a noun and a verb.

Example: police—*n.* an agency that enforces the law

v. to monitor or watch others

1. signal:_____

_____

2. corner: _____

_____

3. station: _____

_____

4. spell:_____

_____

Read the underlined word in each sentence. Determine if it is being used as a noun or a verb.

1. I broke a <u>peddle</u> riding to the store. _____

2. <u>Staple</u> the papers together. _____

3. I will <u>diet</u> tomorrow. _____

4. <u>Raise</u> your hand if you want a hot lunch. _____

5. Bread, flour, and eggs are <u>staples</u>. _____

6. My dad was given a pay <u>raise</u>. _____

7. My family always follows a healthy <u>diet</u>. _____

8. They are going to <u>peddle</u> trinkets at the fair. _____

WRITE ON!

Brainstorm with a classmate and make a list of five other words with multiple meanings. Then, on
separate sheets of paper, use the words in a paragraph on a topic of your choice. Share your paragraph
with the same classmate you worked with to brainstorm the list of words.

Name _____ Date _____

Citing Informational Sources

It is important to credit the **sources of information** used when doing research for a report. A writer should list, or cite, the reference materials used to prepare his or her report. This information is included in the report's bibliography. It can include a variety of sources including books, magazines, newspaper articles, and websites.

When *citing a book*, be sure to include the following information:

- author's name (last name, first name)
- title of book or article
- publisher
- place of publication
- publication date
- pages where information was found

Example: Butler, Tim. How to Crack Your Own Back. Fresno Publishers, Fresno, CA 2008. pp. 208–213.

PRACTICE

Write bibliographic information for two different books.

Book #1

_____

_____

Book #2

_____

_____

Why is it important to give credit to the author or publisher?

_____

_____

WRITE ON!

How would you feel if someone used your research and did not give you credit? _____

_____

What could you do? _____

_____

Name _____   Date _____

Dewey Decimal System

The **Dewey Decimal System** is a way of organizing the non-fiction books within the library. All of the books are assigned a number within a given category. This makes it easy for the patrons to find a particular book and for the librarians to return the book to its correct place.

Dewey Decimal System	
000 Generalities	500 Natural Sciences and Math
100 Philosophy and Psychology	600 Technology and Applied Sciences
200 Religion	700 Arts, Sports, Recreation
300 Social Studies	800 Literature and Rhetoric
400 Languages	900 Geography, History, Biography

PRACTICE

Where would you look to find the following types of books? List the general call number.

1. a Spanish-English dictionary _____

2. a book on algebra _____

3. maps of the world _____

4. an almanac _____

5. a book on engineering _____

6. life story of a movie star _____

7. baseball _____

8. different kinds of art _____

9. religions of the world _____

10. the Civil War _____

11. telephone books _____

12. yoga _____

13. music _____

14. customs in other countries _____

What new categories would you add to the Dewey Decimal system? Why? _____

_____

How are works of fiction found in a library? _____

_____

WRITE ON!

Before the Dewey Decimal system was invented, the books were just placed on any empty shelf space. Which system is better? Why? Explain your answer on a separate sheet of paper.

Name _____   Date _____

Dewey Decimal System

The **Dewey Decimal System** is a way of organizing the non-fiction books within the library. All of the books are assigned a number within a given category. These numbers make it easy for the patrons to find a particular book and for the librarians to return the book to its correct place.

Dewey Decimal System		
500 Natural Sciences and Math		600 Technology and Applied Sciences
510 Math		610 Medicine
520 Astronomy		620 Engineering
530 Physics		630 Agriculture
540 Chemistry		640 Home Economics (cooking, etc.)
550 Earth Sciences		650 Management
560 Paleontology		660 Chemical Engineering
570 Life Sciences		670 Manufacturing
580 Plants		680 Manufacture for Specific Uses
590 Animals		690 Building

PRACTICE

Write the call number for each of the following topics.

1. cactus _____
2. fossils _____
3. cookbook _____
4. types of homes _____
5. stars _____
6. motion _____
7. geology _____
8. periodic table _____
9. oil _____
10. home remedies _____

11. giraffes _____
12. crop rotation _____
13. fuels _____
14. trigonometry _____
15. textiles _____
16. management style _____
17. molecules _____
18. planets _____
19. sewing _____
20. chemotherapy _____

Which topics within each category surprised you?_____
_____
_____

WRITE ON!

If you were to write a book, which category would the book fit into? What information would you cover in the book? Answer these questions in a paragraph on a separate sheet of paper.

Name _____   Date _____

DAILY
Warm-Up 156

Card Catalog

The **card catalog** is used to locate a book within the library. Some card catalogs are computerized. A card catalog can be used to locate a book three different ways:

- by author
- by title
- by subject

Books listed by *author* will contain the following information:

- author's last name, first name
- book title
- place of publication
- publisher
- copyright date
- number of pages
- call number

PRACTICE

Select two books. Write an author card for each book.

Book 1

_____
_____
_____
_____
_____
_____
_____

Book 2

_____
_____
_____
_____
_____
_____
_____

WRITE ON!

How do you go about finding a particular book in the library? Explain your process on a separate sheet of paper. How might a card catalog (paper or computerized) help you find your book?

Name _____ Date _____

Card Catalog

The **card catalog** is used to locate a book within the library. Some card catalogs are computerized. A card catalog can be used to locate a book three different ways:

- by author
- by title
- by subject

All three cards—*title*, *author*, and *subject*—contain the following information:

- author's last name, first name
- book title
- place of publication
- publisher
- copyright date
- number of pages
- call number

When searching by title or subject, the difference is that the title will be first on the title card and the subject will be first on the subject card. See the subject card below.

> **COWBOYS**
> Bullock, Ivan
> I Wish I Were a Cowboy
> World Book Publication in association with Two Can, 1998.
> 24 pages
> Call number: JUN 636.2BUL

PRACTICE

Answer the questions about the subject card above.

1. What is the subject? _____

2. What year was the book published? _____

3. How many pages are in the book? _____

4. What is the author's name? _____

5. What is the title of the book? _____

6. What is the call number? _____

7. Who published the book? _____

8. What do you think the JUN stands for? _____

WRITE ON!

On a separate sheet of paper, write what you think the most important piece of information on the author, subject, or title card might be? Why?

Warm-Up 1 (page 8)
1. verb
2. interjection
3. pronoun
4. adverb
5. adverb
6. conjunction
7. preposition
8. preposition
9. noun
10. pronoun
11. interjection
12. verb
13. noun
14. adjective

Warm-Up 2 (page 9)
Check the eight common nouns for each category.
1. neighbor, desert, summer
2. boys, cars
3. designer
4. family, restaurant
5. appliances, manufacturer
6. school, school
7. principal, truck
8. brothers, skateboards, park
9. recipe, pie
10. event, volcano, year

Warm-Up 3 (page 10)
Check the proper nouns for each topic.
Check the use of proper nouns to complete the story.

Warm-Up 4 (page 11)
1. army
2. atlas
3. band
4. board
5. troop
6. swarm
7. school
8. brood
9. litter
10. cast
11. bunch
12. flock
13. mob
14. pool
15. roll

Warm-Up 5 (page 12)
1. The armada unfurl their sails, raise their anchors, and set sail for new lands.
2. The cast have issues with food, working conditions, and pay.
3. The squad excel in defense, offense, and surprise tactics.
4. The brood sleep, eat, and lay eggs in their nests.
5. The mob enjoy boxing, hopping, and swinging their tails at each other.
6. The bunch were bruised, broken, and split in half.

Warm-Up 6 (page 13)
1. Tess' or Tess's
2. fox's or foxes'
3. Bob's
4. Gus's or Gus'
5. pencil's
6. Sis' or Sis's
7. watch's
8. Ross' or Ross's
9. pillow's
10. bank's
11. anchor's
12. castle's
13. beach's
14. shoe's
15. bowl's
16. bus's or bus'
17. songs'
18. boss' or boss's
19. television's
20. desk's
1. fox's or foxes'
2. bucket's
3. shoes'
4. Dad's

Warm-Up 7 (page 14)
Sample answers:
1. the craftsman
2. Bill and Sue
3. our dog
4. Fluffy
5. a sports car
6. Mr. Dewey
7. Goodman's
8. The Elephant Whisperer
9. Good Viewing
10. Frieda
Part 2
Sewing Brothers Limited
Petite Sewer
Sew So Easy
zig zag, straight, and whip
The Big Bertha
buttons, zippers, and hems
plain and fancy
The Petite Sewer, Sew So Easy, and The Big Bertha

Warm-Up 8 (page 15)
1. deer
2. scarves
3. women
4. fish, fishes
5. elves
6. teeth
7. oxen
8. moose
9. halves
10. wives
11. mice
12. sheep
13. knives
14. men
15. geese
16. feet
1. mice
2. men
3. elves
4. halves
5. wolves
6. people
7. geese
8. knives

Warm-Up 9 (page 16)
1. The burglar sneaks into the dark house.
2. He climbs through the broken window.
3. He triggers the silent alarm.
4. The burglar tip-toes from room to room.
5. He places the valuables into his pillowcase.
6. He climbs down the ladder and his pants catch on a tree branch.
7. He wriggles in vain to get free.
8. The burglar drops the pillowcase to the ground.
9. The police cars pull up to the house.
10. The police officers point their flashlights at the squirming burglar.

Warm-Up 10 (page 17)
1. think
2. smell
3. touch
4. help
7. taste
10. laugh
11. play
12. hug
14. scream
15. see
17. cry
19. feel
Underline the following:
1. jumps
2. takes
3. makes
4. cruises
5. drink
6. teaches
7. chooses
8. calls
9. works
10. tell

Warm-Up 11 (page 18)
1. wrapped
2. watched
3. baked
4. cooked
5. washed
6. kicked
7. cleaned
8. hunted
9. stopped
10. stayed
11. stabbed
12. napped
Suggested rewrite:
I watched tonight's football game. Our team played the best game ever. My brother scored three touchdowns. My cousin tackled two players and punted the ball four times. My family and I cheered and screamed until we lost our voices. It was a great game!

Warm-Up 12 (page 19)
1. caught
2. taught
3. drank
4. built
5. froze
6. stung
7. hid
8. wet
9. wrote
10. sang
11. kept
12. ate
13. set
14. thought
15. sold
16. slid
17. spoke
18. shut
19. said
20. sat
Paragraph corrections:
go/went
buyed/bought
gived/gave
drived/drove
putted/put
goed/went

Warm-Up 13 (page 20)
1. is/was
2. is/was
3. are/were
4. is/was
5. Are/Were
6. is/was
7. are/were
8. is/was
9. is/was
10. is/was

Warm-Up 14 (page 21)
1. The clock will chime on the hour, every hour.
2. The bathtub will hold about 100 gallons of water.
3. The couch will roll on casters.
4. The sun will rise in the east.
5. The golfers will tee off every morning at 6:00 A.M. sharp.

Future tense rewrite sample:
Nina will prepare the journalists for the president's speech. The journalists will take notes and then will sit down on the folding chairs. Soon President Juarez will come out and will stand behind the podium. She will give a short speech and then will answer questions.

Warm-Up 15 (page 22)
Underline sentences: 1, 2, 3, 5, 6, 10
Check the sentence in the future progressive tense.

Warm-Up 16 (page 23)
Underline sentences: 1, 2, 3, 5, 6, 9, 10
Sentence Corrections:
4. The agents will have searched the rooms looking for the missing money.
7. Will you have seen Zoe before the show ends?
8. I will have been to ten Moonlight Socials since January.

Warm-Up 17 (page 24)
Underline sentences: 1, 2, 3, 5, 7, 10
Check the additional sentences in the future perfect progressive tense.

Warm-Up 18 (page 25)
1. more superficial
2. hungrier
3. thirstier
4. more natural
5. more embarrassed
6. dirtier
7. more magical
8. grumpier
9. more virtuous
10. steeper

Paragraph corrections:
1. tallyer/taller
2. heavyer/heavier
3. largeer/larger
4. biger/bigger
5. bluyer/bluer
6. longerer/longer

Warm-Up 19 (page 26)
1. uglier
2. balder
3. rougher
4. whiter
5. healthier
6. choosier
7. shorter
8. wilder
9. more ferocious
10. chunkier
11. prettier
12. clearer
13. quieter
14. braver
15. more unbelievable

Warm-Up 20 (page 27)
1. richest
2. most poisonous
3. most powerful
4. most outrageous
5. silliest
6. most prestigious
7. most glamorous
8. prettiest
9. most ramshackle
10. most repellant
11. roughest
12. sickest
13. most flattering
14. safest

Warm-Up 21 (page 28)
good; better; best
bad; worse; worst
less; lesser/fewer; least
much, many, some; more; most
far; farther; farthest
    or far; further; furthest.
Check the additional sentences.

Warm-Up 22 (page 29)
1. dozen 12
2. two 2
3. thirty 30
4. ten 10
5. one 1
6. eight 8
7. nine million 9,000,000
8. three 3
9. one million 1,000,000
10. thirteen 13
11. two hundred 200
12. twenty-four 24
13. seven 7
14. sixty-four 64
15. twelve 12
16. fifteen 15

Adjectives in paragraph:
twelfth
eleven
one, two
three
two
one
dozen

Warm-Up 23 (page 30)
1. many
2. much
3. some
4. a lot
5. plenty
6. enough
7. all
8. few
9. any
10. many
11. each
12. all
13. each, every
14. some

Paragraph indefinite adjectives:
a lot
several
few
more

Warm-Up 24 (page 31)
1. warm and sunny
2. fabulous
3. scared
4. hard worker
5. brothers
6. tough competitor
7. fastest typist
8. delicious
9. terrible
10. naughty girl
11. very sick
12. great leader
Check the predicate adjectives in the additional sentences.

Warm-Up 25 (page 32)
1. late
2. early
3. here
4. very
5. early
6. yesterday
7. last
8. quickly
9. often
10. slowly
11. there
12. eerily
13. soundlessly
14. twice
15. endlessly
16. daily
17. nightly
18. roughly
19. regularly
20. ominously

Warm-Up 26 (page 33)
Sample sentences:
1. Gary ran faster than Lily.
2. Nicholas hit the ball harder than Anna.
3. The sloth moved more slowly than the snail.
4. The whiskers felt rougher than the sandpaper.
5. Dad snored more loudly than Grandpa.
6. Sister sang more softly than Momma to the baby.
7. The dancers leaped more gracefully than the frog.
8. The sugar tasted sweeter than the honey.
9. The tiny package was wrapped more beautifully than the bigger present.
10. Tommy played more quietly than Megan.

Warm-Up 27 (page 34)
Sample sentences:
1. The baby chortled most happily of all.
2. The anesthesiologist scrubbed the most carefully of all.
3. The doily was knit the most delicately of all.
4. The handbag was sewn most carefully of all.
5. The old house cat mewed the most pitifully of all.
6. Grandma drove the slowest of all.
7. The dandelions grew the quickest of all.

ANSWER KEY (cont.)

Warm-Up 28 (page 35)
Sample sentences:
1. Greg lives near Grandma.
2. Jose arrived later than Kenneth.
3. Mr. Davidson drove the farthest of all.
4. Michelle lives near the park.
5. Jay lost more weight than Liam.
6. My sister has a lot of money.
7. Janine arrived later than Tim.
8. Cass did the best of all.

Warm-Up 29 (page 36)
Check that the sentences are appropriate for each type of interjection.

Warm-Up 30 (page 37)
1. Get this
   I won
   Oh, no
2. Well
   Yes
   What
   Oh well
3. Awesome
   Hurray
4. Wow
   Yippee
5. Congratulations
   Well
6. Touchdown
   Hurray

Warm-Up 31 (page 38)
Underline the following prepositional phrases:
1. with his hands; in spite of the rule
2. to the very top; of the tree
3. of the computers; in the building
4. in addition to
5. to the bottom
6. in the parking garage
7. all around the world
8. in the heart of the Central Valley; for its agricultural economy
9. to Paula
10. in many hit movies

Warm-Up 32 (page 39)
Check the sentences for prepositional phrases.

Warm-Up 33 (page 40)
1. T   On Sunday
2. T   around lunchtime
3. T   within ten days
4. beside the front door
5. T   During a snowstorm
6. T   Until dinnertime
7. to the other side
8. T   by 2:00 P.M.
9. For some students
10. T   on Tuesday morning
11. T   at 10:00 A.M.
12. by the river
13. to the mall
14. Inside the squirrel's home
15. at the hotel

Warm-Up 34 (page 41)
2. to the grocery store
3. beneath the couch
4. Over the hill
5. onto the escalator
6. under the potted plant
8. into the haunted house
10. below the stove
11. onto the train
12. through this door
14. into the restricted area
15. toward the historical monument

Warm-Up 35 (page 42)
Sample sentences:
1. I went on vacation to Spain, but my sister went on vacation to England.
2. Olive is very tall, so she plays basketball.
3. The dog barked all night and the cat hid.
4. The train traveled quickly, but it did not make it to the next stop on time.
5. The gift is not for you, nor is it for Sheila.
6. The cupcakes were delicious and the cookies were divine.
7. Alex has blue eyes and brown hair.
8. The playground is full of children, but the cafeteria is empty.
9. The book is good, but it is long.

Warm-Up 36 (page 43)
1. but
2. so
3. so
5. or/and
6. but/yet
7. so/and

4. but/yet
but not a sunroof
and saved his money
and he did

Warm-Up 37 (page 44)
1. and
2. or
3. and
4. and
5. but
6. or
7. but
8. or/and
9. or/and
10. for/because/ since

Warm-Up 38 (page 45)
We could either go to camp or spend the summer with my grandparents.
Both my brother and I like camp and we would get to see all of our old camp buddies.
But my brother and I also like to visit my grandparents.
If we go to camp, we can either sleep in a tent or in a cabin.
If we stay with my grandparents, we can neither sleep in a tent nor in a cabin.
Not only is this a difficult decision, but also one we don't want to make!
Check the sentences for correlative conjunctions.
1. both–and, not only–but also, as–as
2. either–or, neither–nor, whether–or

Warm-Up 39 (page 46)
1. He works at night at the factory.
2. It was made by a famous abstract artist.
3. They issued a challenge.
4. He built the dining table and chairs.
5. Her hair is really blonde.
6. He eats breakfast every morning.
7. He (or she) is unable to predict the future.
8. We are both trying out for the same part in the play.
9. He filled his pockets with frogs.
10. It is a common problem during the colder months.

Warm-Up 40 (page 47)
1. the marathon   it
2. Grandma Rose   her
3. the mailbox   it
4. Callie and me   us

5. the game   it
6. Mr. and Mrs. Boyd   them
7. the box   it
8. the river   it
9. the baby   him/her
10. the letter   it
Paragraph changes:
gardening shed   it
garden   it
weeds   them
the young seedlings   them
soil   it
plants   them
plants   them
plants   them
tools   them
tools   them

Warm-Up 41 (page 48)
Where
What
Which
Whichever
Check the questions for each interrogative pronoun.

Warm-Up 42 (page 49)
1. That/This
2. these
3. That/This
4. Those/These
5. This/That
6. this/that/these/those
7. this/that/these/those

Warm-Up 43 (page 50)
Answers will vary based on the demonstrative pronoun chosen.
1. these/*closer* or those/*further away*
2. this/*closer* or that/*further away*
3. These/*closer* or Those/*further away*
4. This/*closer* or That/*further away*
5. this/*closer* or that/*further away*
6. this/*closer* or that/*further away* or these/*closer* or those/*further away*
7. this/*closer* or that/*further away* or these/*closer* or those/*further away*
8. These/*closer* or Those/*further away*
9. This/*closer* or That/*further away*
10. This/*closer* or That/*further away*
11. These/*closer* or Those/*further away*

12. this/*closer* or that/*further away*

Warm-Up 44 (page 51)
1. Our boots and skis are in the garage.
2. This is their yard sale.
3. The dolls are hers.
4. Her room is always as neat as a pin.
5. His motorcycle is in tip-top shape.
6. The limousine is for her.
7. The paintings were hers.
8. Her/My sunglasses were designed by Sam and Joan.
9. His bowl is over there.
10. The computer is mine.

Warm-Up 45 (page 52)
its kind
her machine
ours
its attachments
her craft room
Check each sentence for a possessive pronoun.

Warm-Up 46 (page 53)
1. anybody
2. everything
3. everyone
4. Nothing
5. somebody
6. Everybody
7. No one
8. Somebody
Check the sentences for each indefinite pronoun.

Warm-Up 47 (page 54)
1. (George) himself
2. (You) yourself
3. (They) themselves
4. (I) myself
5. (dog) itself
6. (boys) themselves
7. (mom) herself
8. (cat) itself
9. (Mom) herself
10. (Claire) herself

Paragraph corrections:
by *himself*
herself a snack
himself in the head

Warm-Up 48 (page 55)
Underline the following sentences: 1, 2, 3, 6, 8
1. [He] put cheese on his pizza.
2. [Bonnie] peeled the pepperoni off her pizza.
3. [Sammy] slid it out of the oven.
4. [Theo] tossed the dough.
5. [The delivery person] carried the pizza up the stairs.
6. [She and I] sprinkled the toppings on the pie.

Warm-Up 49 (page 56)
Moosie had a litter of puppies. There ~~was~~ *were* ten puppies in the litter. There were six girl and four boy puppies. The biggest puppy ~~were~~ *was* named Piggy. Piggy was twice the size of the other puppies. The smallest puppy ~~were~~ *was* a boy. He liked to sleep on his back. One of the puppies was named Lightning because his white patch of fur looked like a streak of lightning. Another puppy ~~have~~ *had* a white patch of fur that looked like a flame.
1. The ladder needs to be moved.
2. The paint is still wet.
3. Have you ever been to the zoo?
4. There are dogs next door.
5. Chief, my dog, escapes all the time.

Warm-Up 50 (page 57)
1. The computers are on the fritz again.
2. The boys love the little dog.
3. The science-fiction movies are earning rave reviews.
4. The cherry pies are cooling on the counter.
5. The managers of the store were very friendly.
6. no predicate
7. no subject
8. no subject
Check the rewrites for subject-predicate agreement.

Warm-Up 51 (page 58)
1. walter does not work very often.
2. everything adds up to twelve.
3. the author finished writing the book.
4. mr. stucky is getting married.
5. cheryl runs up and down the stairs for exercise.
6. robin and dave host a weekly talk show.
7. the movie was pretty spooky.
8. the chocolate flower tasted delicious.
9. the clock beeps every half hour.
10. mrs. davis bought a new washer and dryer.

Josiah ~~were~~ *was* trying out for the school's chess team. He ~~has~~ *had* to play a chess match against the team's coach, ms. Warner. josiah made the opening move. Soon, Ms. Warner and Josiah ~~was~~ *were* locked in battle. the chess match ended in a draw. Josiah became the newest member of the chess team.

Warm-Up 52 (page 59)
Check the declarative sentences for each topic 1–5.
The following sentences should have been crossed out:
Have you ever been mountain climbing?
You are probably wondering, "Where do I go to take a mountain climbing class?"
Why should people bother to take a class?
Why not go ahead and give it a try?

Warm-Up 53 (page 60)
1. When is it going to rain?
2. Why is Benita always late for work?
3. Why was the mummy wrapped in cloth?
4. Have you ever been to Egypt?
5. Do the Johnsons live in the two-story house?
6. Did the wind blow the table over?
7. What caused the building to collapse?
8. How is calculus different from geometry?
Check the interrogatory sentences.

Warm-Up 54 (page 61)
Sample responses:
1. Does Marie take a vitamin every morning?
2. Does Wilbur want to be a detective when he grows up?
3. Did Dad decide to grow a beard?
4. Is chartreuse her favorite color? / What is her favorite color?
5. Did the furniture store have a spring sale?
6. Is the name of the new school Fremont Elementary?
7. Did they name the new baby Madeline Marie?
8. Is Europe home to many royal families?
9. Does Cherise create magnificent pieces of silver jewelry?
10. Is the book on the bestsellers' list again?
11. Why is Marcus wearing a garish purple tie?
12. Does Ivan like to brush his teeth?

Warm-Up 55 (page 62)
Sample commands:
1. Do your homework every night.
2. Be careful with your lunch money.
3. Do not eat candy.
4. Paint the deck.
5. Pack your bags for the trip.
6. Watch your little brother.
7. Walk the dogs.
8. Write a letter to Great Aunt Myrtle.
9. Make a pitcher of lemonade.
10. Stop making that squeaking noise.

Warm-Up 56 (page 63)
Answers will vary. Check the responses.

Warm-Up 57 (page 64)
Add exclamation points to the following sentences: 3, 5, 7, 8, 9, 10, 11, 15.
Place an **E** at the beginning.
Add periods to the following declarative sentences: 1, 2, 4, 6, 12, 13, 14.
Place a **D** at the beginning.

Warm-Up 58 (page 65)
1. Don't look at your neighbor's paper. Imperative
2. Who studied for this test? Interrogative
3. Raise your hand. Imperative
4. Mario earned the highest score! Exclamatory
5. The test has twenty questions. Declarative
6. Are you ready? Interrogative
7. Write your name at the top of the paper. Imperative

Warm-Up 59 (page 66)
1. interrogative
2. exclamatory
3. imperative
4. interrogative
5. exclamatory
6. declarative
7. declarative
8. exclamatory
9. interrogative
10. interrogative
11. declarative
12. exclamatory
13. exclamatory
14. imperative
15. imperative
16. interrogative
17. interrogative
18. interrogative
19. declarative
20. declarative

Warm-Up 60 (page 67)
Suggested corrections:

Paragraph 1

my shoes are killing my feet! what was I thinking? i should have listened to my mom, she wanted me to get something sensible, like sneakers, instead i bought the mile-high platforms, never again!

Paragraph 2

in the middle of the night, we awoke to a weird ringing sound, where was the ringing coming from? mom checked in the bathroom, dad checked in the garage, my sister and i looked in the living room, finally, mom found what was making the ringing noise, it was the kitchen timer, guess where mom found the timer, it was in her purse!

Warm-Up 61 (page 68)
1. After the game was over,
2. When he lost out on the story,
3. ,which is made in Germany,
4. ,which is filled with many living things,
5. When you finish the test,
Dependent clauses in the paragraph:
When I was your age
on the way home
When I was knee-high to a grasshopper
Way back when
when he was young
as you can see

Warm-Up 62 (page 69)
1. I will call you
2. put on your shoes
3. Sherry makes her bed
4. The alarm rings
5. the windows are filthy
6. Barnaby does really well
7. Garth fell into the shallow end of the pool
8. all of the kids came down with chicken pox
9. The tree grew tall and strong
10. the dog gets so excited
11. We put on our snowsuits and go out and play
12. the team was in good spirits
Check the independent clauses and the response to the question.

Warm-Up 63 (page 70)
1. independent
2. independent
3. independent
4. dependent
5. dependent
Dependent clauses in paragraph:
which are located throughout the valley
Each day at dawn
At each machine
who pay with dollar bills
where he deposits the days receipts
When he returns home
Check the dependent and independent clauses.

Warm-Up 64 (page 71)
1. to reach **v.**
2. a sad person **n.**; to vomit **v.**
3. to draw **v.**
4. a boat **n.**
5. to retrieve or get **v.**
6. to inhabit **v.**; a location **n.**
7. to show off **v.**
8. a trip **n.**
9. make (someone) feel intimidated or apprehensive **v.**
10. sickly, thin **adj.**
Paragraph answers:
gaunt
jaunt
ketch
haunt
sketch

Warm-Up 65 (page 72)
1. twinge
2. brought
3. binge
4. sought
5. cringe
6. thought
7. hinge
8. ought
9. fought
10. bought
Paragraph answers:
twinge
sought
cringe
thought
tinge

Warm-Up 66 (page 73)
1. sound
2. taught
3. could
4. caught
5. pound
6. mound
7. daughter
8. Would
9. around
10. found
11. ground
12. hound
13. round

Warm-Up 67 (page 74)
1. aunt, ant
2. foul, fowl
3. groan, grown
4. boar, bore
5. tow, toe
6. role, roll
7. rose, rows
8. Matt, mat
9. rung, wrung
10. Would, wood
11. you, ewe
12. way, weigh
13. thrown, throne
14. too, two, to
15. sent, cent
16. sail, sale

Warm-Up 68 (page 75)
Check the sentences using pairs of homophones.

Paragraph answers:
son
sun
scent
sent
eight
ate
inn
in
know
no

Warm-Up 69 (page 76)
1. Our
2. our
3. Our
4. hour
5. hour
6. hour
7. Our
8. hour
9. hour
10. Our
11. our
12. hour

Paragraph homophones:
hour
our
hour
Our
our

Warm-Up 70 (page 77)
1. They're
2. there
3. Their
4. Their
5. There
6. Their
7. They're
8. their
9. there
10. They're

Check the three sentences.

Warm-Up 71 (page 78)
1. Two
2. two
3. too
4. too
5. two
6. to
7. too
8. two
9. to
10. too
11. two
12. two
13. to
14. to
15. to

Check the three sentences.

Warm-Up 72 (page 79)
Possible responses:
1. to flatten; a vegetable
2. a piece of jewelry; to circle around
3. something to write on; an intern
4. a flowering plant; remain silent
5. what a duck says; a phony doctor (slang)
6. balanced; a place where horses sleep
7. the side of a hill; a place of business (money)
8. a desire for something; Japanese money

9. a type of tree; to fix up
10. used to fill a tank; to inflate with air

Warm-Up 73 (page 80)
Possible responses:
1. the underground growth system of a tree
2. a player on a baseball team
3. period of time occuring now
4. a group of fish
5. a fenced area
6. the answer sheet
7. part of the body formed by a person when sitting
8. a structure dug into the ground to hold rain water

Warm-Up 74 (page 81)
Possible responses:
1. bow: to bend at the waist
   bow: a decoratively tied ribbon
2. tear: rip
   tear: the drop that falls from the eye when you cry
3. desert: a hot, dry place
   desert: to leave
4. close: to shut
   close: to be near
5. dove: a bird
   dove: to jump in head first
6. minute: tiny
   minute: sixty seconds
7. object: to complain
   object: an item

Warm-Up 75 (page 82)
1. to oppose
2. to write down
3. not legal
4. to delay
5. moving air
6. to turn
7. sum of past achievements

Underline the following:
1. sow, sow
2. row, row
3. sewer, sewer
4. tear, tear
5. minute, minute

Warm-Up 76 (page 83)
Suggested responses:
1. night
2. smell
3. finger
4. woman
5. pants

6. head/hair
7. cold
8. cast
9. pot
10. hands
11. scale
12. full
13. oven
14. dog
15. bear/lion/etc.

Warm-Up 77 (page 84)
Suggested answers:
1. sail—What each item does
2. French—The language spoken in each country
3. listen—How each item is enjoyed
4. hot—The temperature of each item
5. pounds/weight—What each item measures
6. twenty-five cents—Value of each item
7. twenty—Numerical order
8. egg—Animal and product
9. ice—What each house is made of
10. flies—How each animal moves
11. nest—Where each animal lives
12. ink/paper—What each item needs
13. hearing aide—What each organ might need
14. cereal/grain—Food group
15. wild—Animals that live in each location

Warm-Up 78 (page 85)
1. speak, declare
2. amazing, astounding
3. attractive, good-looking
4. beat, conquer
5. hue, tint
6. acquaintance, neighbor
7. act, compete
8. contest, match
9. hog, swine
10. novel, volume

Suggested synonyms:
1. buddy; companion
2. attempt
3. hog; boar
4. devour; gobble
5. chooses
6. hue; shade; tint

Warm-Up 79 (page 86)
Sample synonym changes:
1. I dreamed that a <u>creature</u> was chasing me.
2. I jangled my keys as I <u>ambled</u> to my motorcycle.
3. I rode quickly down the <u>road</u>.
4. I <u>tapped</u> the horn to warn people about the danger.
5. The monster <u>thudded</u> down the street behind me.
6. It kept <u>snarling</u> at me.
7. I <u>banged</u> my motorcycle.
8. I landed face-first in a <u>gob</u> of wet cement.
9. When I woke up, I had my pillow <u>crammed</u> in my mouth.
10. What a <u>wild</u> dream!

Warm-Up 80 (page 87)
Possible answers:
1. inept; unable
2. destroy; ruin
3. purchase; buy
4. bold; outgoing
5. beautiful; pretty
6. happy; joyful
7. lackadaisical; irresponsible
8. disorganized; messy
9. respect
10. placid

Possible paragraph antonyms:
many-few
remember-forget
girl-boy
She-He
new-old
whisper-yell

Warm-Up 81 (page 88)
Possible answers:
1. ingest—regurgitate
2. sporadic—orderly; systematic
3. divide—join
4. personal—public
5. stretchy—rigid
6. happy—dissatisfied
7. uninspired—exciting
8. thrifty—extravagant
9. distort—shape
10. rough—smooth
11. enemy—patriot
12. funny—sad

Warm-Up 82 (page 89)
1. synonyms
2. antonyms
3. synonyms
4. synonyms
5. antonyms
6. antonyms
7. antonyms
8. synonyms
9. antonyms
10. antonyms
11. synonyms
12. synonyms
13. antonyms
14. antonyms

Possible synonyms for paragraph:
see—view
costume—outfit
tall—high; giant; large
big—huge
mean—unkind

Warm-Up 83 (page 90)
1. changed
2. to save
3. first
4. move
5. many
6. to pull out of place

Warm-Up 84 (page 91)
Possible definitions:
1. same outfits
2. to speak the story
3. the hand-written story
4. things he wants to know
5. many people in a city
1. popular
2. requests
3. narrative
4. manufactures
5. reform

Warm-Up 85 (page 92)
1. turbulence—bumpy weather conditions in the air/atmosphere
2. similar—same appearance; alike
3. maternity—mother's (floor)
4. suburbs—outside of the city
5. textile—weavers, makers of fabric
6. texture—feel of the fabric
7. simultaneously—at the same time
8. lunar—of the moon
9. disturb—not to bother

10. urban—city areas
11. maternal—acting motherly
12. similes—like, comparing

Warm-Up 86 (page 93)
1. photographer—person who takes pictures
2. biologist—person who studies life
3. arachnophobia—fear of spiders
4. thermos—container for liquids
5. telephoto—long-distance camera lens
6. claustrophobic—fear of closed in spaces
7. thermometer—measures temperature
8. bibliophile—book lover
9. cardiologist—heart doctor
10. thermal—warm

Underline the following:
thermal
thermos
thermometer
thermostat

Warm-Up 87 (page 94)
1. words that are the same
2. person who fixes machines
3. measures in one hundreds
4. earth study
5. long-distance letters
1. grammar
2. thermometer
3. mechanism
4. geometry
5. antonym

Warm-Up 88 (page 95)
Possible responses:
1. time order
2. ring of wind
3. star traveler
4. speech
5. person who works with teeth
1. chronometer: instrument for measuring time
2. orthodontics: tooth study
3. bicycles: two-wheeled cycles

Warm-Up 89 (page 96)
1. unable/not able
2. preview/see before
3. distrust/not trust
4. preset/set before
5. unlock/to not lock

1. dislike
2. rewind
3. retest
4. reassemble
5. reappear
6. review
7. prepay
8. unassembled
9. distaste
10. retie
re (built)
re (packaged)
re (assemble)
dis (cover)
pre (sorted)
re (sorted)
dis (assembled)
re (turn)
pre (assembled)

Warm-Up 90 (page 97)
1. foreword/the words at the front of the book
2. forewarned/warned ahead of time
3. incomplete/not finished
4. forerunner/runner at the front in the race
5. inadequate/not adequate
6. incapable/not capable
7. foretell/tell before it happens
8. encroach/intrude upon
9. encode/put into code
10. informal/not formal
1. inanimate
2. inarticulate
3. forewarn
4. inadequate
5. enclose

Warm-Up 91 (page 98)
1. predates/before the dates of an event or period
2. promote/make ready for
3. preoperative/before the operation
4. prohibits/does not allow
5. postpaid/paid after
6. posthumously/given after death
7. prepaid/paid before use
8. probable/likely
Underline the following:
premiere
promoting
Postscript
promised
preview

posthypnotic

Warm-Up 92 (page 99)
Possible responses:
1. more than human
2. more than natural
3. among a group or organization
4. more than fine
5. within a sport
6. in addition to or beyond the curriculum
7. more than a star
Check the sentences.
Underline the following:
intramural
extraordinary
superdome
supermarket
superstar
extracurricular

Warm-Up 93 (page 100)
1. full of joy
2. person who gardens
3. full of wonder
4. to do something horrible
5. full of grace
6. a person who rides
7. person who teaches
8. how often something is done
9. full of hate
10. to do something in a safe manner
1. singers/people who sing
2. handful/fill the hand
3. dancer/person who dances
4. gently/it is done in a gentle way
5. lawyer/person who practices the law
6. skater/person who skates

Warm-Up 94 (page 101)
1. fashionable
2. visible
3. capable
4. horrible
5. terrible
6. advisable
7. honorable
8. suitable
9. edible
10. unbelievable
11. dependable
12. incredible
13. unbearable
14. desirable
15. comfortable

Warm-Up 95 (page 102)

1. rage
2. bridge
3. hedge
4. page
5. stage
6. sage
7. ledge
8. ridge
9. dredge
10. pledge

Underline the following:

edge
wedge
manage
dredge
bridge
pledged

Warm-Up 96 (page 103)

1. confusion
2. vacation
3. fraction
4. question
5. permission
6. Action
7. motion
8. production
9. section
10. invention
11. sensation
12. mansion
13. extension
14. vision
15. nation
16. collection

Warm-Up 97 (page 104)

1. ninety
2. forty
3. temperature
4. theories
5. weird
6. their
7. since
8. shoulder
9. library
10. friend
11. license
12. all right/alright
13. believe
14. niece
15. neighbor

Warm-Up 98 (page 105)

1. greatful/grateful
2. eqipt/equipped
3. arguement/argument
4. attitud/attitude
5. devide/divide
6. stores/stories
7. favrite/favorite

8. truely/truly
9. redikulus/ridiculous
10. separate/separate
11. restrant/restaurant
12. yeld/yield

Underlined words and corrections:

1. wif/with
2. frend/friend
3. pickt/picked
4. delishus /delicious
5. tastey /tasty
6. payd/paid
7. packt/packed
8. groseries/groceries
9. grate/great
10. desert/dessert

Warm-Up 99 (page 106)

Paragraph 1—finally, coming, forty, carried, clothes, ready
Paragraph 2—family, business, restaurant, meant, exercise, match

Warm-Up 100 (page 107)

1. deere/dear
2. studyied/studied
3. realy/really
4. mist/missed
5. kan/can
6. mispeld/misspelled
7. mowntan/mountain
8. no/know
9. culd/could
10. hav/have
11. spelr/speller
12. stude/study
13. git/get

Warm-Up 101 (page 108)

1. rule 4/ship-yard
2. rule 4/dream-y
3. rule 2/o-pen
4. rule 4/bed-spread
5. rule 1/pil-low
6. rule 4/flow-ers
7. rule 1 or 3/mid-dle
8. rule 1/par-cel
9. rule 4/bath-tub
10. rule 3/sim-ple

Warm-Up 102 (page 109)

1. wax
2. guard
3. squash
4. buckle
5. plug
6. school
7. pinch
8. touched

Warm-Up 103 (page 110)

1. At the last minute
2. To speak badly of others
3. To listen carefully
4. To be easily done
5. To begin the trip
6. To be lazy; spend one's time watching television
7. Won't commit to a decision

Check the use of idioms.

1. To move slowly
2. To be seriously ill

Warm-Up 104 (page 111)

1. They don't agree
2. To finish early
3. To call the person
4. Not paying attention to what is going on around him
5. Not much of a chance of passing the test
6. She is crazy
7. She is very slow
8. The person knows what looks good
9. To not give the person an honest answer
10. A person is in a bad mood

Warm-Up 105 (page 112)

1. really lays it on thick—Overdoes the praise
2. go to the dogs—not taken care of
3. fishy—suspicious
4. getting in my hair—bothering me
5. shooting off his mouth—speaking without thinking first
6. pay through the nose—pay an exorbitant price
7. by ear—taking the day as it comes
8. all thumbs—clumsy
9. high and dry—abandoned
10. selling me short—underestimating me

Warm-Up 106 (page 113)

1. like a computer—very smart
2. as stubborn as a mule—very stubborn (rigid)
3. as thin as a pencil—very skinny
4. as happy as a clam—very joyful

5. like a caterpillar in a cocoon—wrapped up tightly
6. like a fly at a picnic—went all over
7. like a pigsty—very messy

First paragraph similes:
like a wet hen
as mad as a hornet
as flat as a pancake
as happy as a pig in a poke
like a fairy godmother
Second paragraph similes:
as heavy as a concrete block
as old as the hills
as light as a feather
Check similes.

Warm-Up 107 (page 114)

1. as poor as church mice—to not have any money
2. like a book—her face tells how she is feeling as helpful
3. as helpful as a square wheel—not helpful at all
4. like talking to a brick wall–the person is not willing to listen to a different opinion
5. like a waterfall—the water flowed/gushed out
6. like he had been through a war and lost—to be disheveled and tired looking
7. like golf balls —to be large in size
8. as hard as cement—to be hard to eat or serve
9. like a throne—to be massive and regal in size
10. like a king—to treat in a grand manner

Check similes.

Warm-Up 108 (page 115)
Possible answers:
1. The dog is as big as a pony.
2. The old car works as well as a fish out of water.
3. Phil is like a grumpy bear.
4. She dances as gracefully as a swan.
5. The fluffy pillow is like a cloud.

Paragraph similes:
like a three-alarm fire
like a little mouse
like you were just born
like a hot potato
like a newly-minted penny

Paragraph rewrite:
The telephone was ringing. Barb answered the phone before it rang again. On the phone was a fast-talking salesperson trying to sell a vitamin. Barb said, "No thanks," and dropped the phone. Barb went back to waxing the floor.

Check response to the question.

Warm-Up 109 (page 116)
Check the similes 1–4.
Underlined similes:
like a bass drum in a parade
like a grocery list
like a champion racehorse

Warm-Up 110 (page 117)
1. difficult to get along with
2. the reception is not very good
3. to be very proud of oneself
4. to have dirty ears; to not hear well
5. to have a very short attention span
6. to have large eyes; one's eyes open wide
7. to be very hot
8. to have a thick layer of make-up on
9. to have a large number of overgrown plants
10. to have long, sharp nails

Warm-Up 111 (page 118)
Possible interpretations:
1. stronger than an ox—He is very strong.
2. chocolate bricks—The brownies were hard and inedible.

3. straighter than a ruler—She has good posture.
4. smoother than a purring cat—The car's engine has a smooth, rhythmic sound.
5. worse than a chicken's—The handwriting is very scratchy and hard to read.

Check the metaphors for each chosen topic.

Warm-Up 112 (page 119)
1. an old dinosaur—very old
2. heart of gold—very nice
3. a lifesaver—She is very helpful.
4. a clown—Chase is funny.
5. faster than an adding machine—she can add very quickly
6. older than the hills—been around forever

Check the metaphors.

Warm-Up 113 (page 120)
Check the metaphors.
Metaphors underlined:
older than the hills
larger than a tractor's tires
heavier than an elephant
Similes circled:
like an army ant
like a horse

Warm-Up 114 (page 121)
1. The sun wrapped me in its warmth.
2. When milk was poured over the cereal, the cereal popped and crackled.
3. The fried chicken was speaking to me, saying, "Eat me!"
4. The newspaper was wrinkled and yellowed with age.
5. The mud clung mightily to his shoes and pants.
6. The cabin welcomed us home after a hard day of hiking.
7. The clay took shape within my hands.
8. The sapling bent and twined gracefully around the trellis.
9. The pencil's sharp point stabbed and poked at the paper.
10. The puppy snuggled and

sighed in my arms.
11. The wood glowed with a warm, rosy sheen.
12. The ants attacked the bread and carried it home for their queen.

Check the sentences using personification for each topic.

Warm-Up 115 (page 122)
After the long trip, coming home was like hugging an old friend.
Some of the clothes were so dirty, they could stand up by themselves.
At the twist of the dial, the washer whirred to life, stripping the dirt from the clothes.
The suitcases were lined up as if they were little soldiers waiting for their marching orders.
The couch sighed as it accepted Marcie's weight.
The turtle nibbled neatly at the sweet blades of grass until he had his fill.
When done, he licked his lips as if satisfied with his delightful vegetarian snack.
After a little nap, the rested turtle peeked out of his shell before sticking his head out, stretched his limbs, and began the long journey back to his cozy home.

Check the sentences examples of personification.

Warm-Up 116 (page 123)
Answers will vary.
Paragraph personifications:
ball flew swiftly
crowd roared
scoreboard came alive
lights flashing
firecrackers shooting
court jumped and jiggled

Warm-Up 117 (page 124)
Check the alliterations for each animal.

Warm-Up 118 (page 125)
Possible answers:
1. quack quack
2. crack; crash
3. toot; honk
4. clap
5. ruff; grrrrrrowl; bark
6. cheep-cheep; tweet-tweet; caw-caw
7. purr

8. creak
9. ding; rrrrring
10. roar
11. oink-oink
12. vroom; vroooom

Warm-Up 119 (page 126)
Check the proper nouns for each topic.
Capitalize the following:
Monday
Fantastic Fast Food
Fantastic Fast Food
Palm Avenue
Hemlock Avenue
Fantastic Fast Food

Warm-Up 120 (page 127)
Paragraph 1
Monday
Mrs. Givens
Friday
Paragraph 2
Christmas or Winter Vacation
mid-December
January
During
Paragraph 3
English
Emma
Spring Fling Fashion Show
(The) Harrisburg Press
LBL Evening News

Warm-Up 121 (page 128)
1. Every student needs a pencil box filled with pencils, erasers, markers, rulers, and crayons.
2. In case of an emergency, every child should know his or her phone number, the parents' home and work numbers, home address, emergency meeting place, and emergency phone numbers.
3. I am wearing a jacket, scarf, mittens, and a hat.
4. Many men now go to day spas for special treatments including manicures, pedicures, facials, and massages.
5. To make a fantastic peanut butter and jelly sandwich, you will need bread, a knife, peanut butter, jelly, and a plate.

Warm-Up 122 (page 129)
1. Tuesday, January 5, 2010
2. March 2, 2009
3. Friday, September 25, 2009
4. Wednesday, January 27, 2010
5. February 14, 2008
6. November 30, 2009
7. Thursday, October 2, 2008
8. April 2007
9. Saturday, May 24, 2008
10. June 21, 2009

Commas for passage:
Friday, April 4, 2009
May 9, 2009
Tuesday, June 9
Wednesday, June 10
Thursday, June 11, 2009

Warm-Up 123 (page 130)
Letter #1
June 2, 2005
Dear Grandma,
Next time, let's make some pumpkin pies.
Love,
Letter #2
December 1, 2007
Dear Santa Claus,
I took care of my little brother and sister, raked leaves, kept my room clean, and washed the dishes.
Your little helper,

Warm-Up 124 (page 131)
1. Alaska is the largest state, but it has a small population.
2. The car had a brand new battery, yet it would not start.
3. It was icy cold outside, but inside the home was warm and cozy.
4. The dogs look fierce and dangerous, but they are friendly and lovable.
5. I brought a cold lunch today, so I won't need to use my lunch card.
6. Jonah's favorite color is red, but he also likes blue.
7. Jenna loves all kinds of frogs, so she has decorated her house with frogs.
8. Paul likes to save all of his change, and he keeps the coins separated into different jars.
9. Mom has an important business meeting today, so she wore her "power suit."
10. The 6th grade students are wearing hats with tassels, for they are graduating today.

Warm-Up 125 (page 132)
1. Chaz's black horse is named Blackie.
2. Michelle's desk is the messiest in school!
3. Brent's film is in the Valley Film Festival.
4. Our newspaper boy's red bike is a Super Speedy.
5. Alex's coat is made of fake fur.
6. In the fashion show, Jean's dress was pink.
7. The teddy bear's bow fell off.
8. The judge's gavel belongs on the desk.
9. Grandma's beach house overlooks the ocean.
10. Max's luggage is red and gold.

Warm-Up 126 (page 133)
Possible changes:
1. This weekend we went to my friend's house.
2. Bob's green house is about three houses down the street.
3. Our first step was borrowing tools from Bob's dad and uncle.
4. Bob's sister, Jenna, came out of the house when we were done.

Warm-Up 127 (page 134)
1. The children's hospital is located in Madera.
2. The men's restroom is on the right.
3. The band members' instrument cases are on the bus.
4. The women's society made the blankets.
5. The painters' brushes were cleaned.
6. The ducks' feathers dropped to the ground.
7. The people's donations were greatly needed.
8. The boys' jackets were on the floor.
9. The birds' singing is beautiful.

Warm-Up 128 (page 135)
1. The fluffy dog is Martha and George's.
2. The saddle is for my Aunt and Uncle's horse.
3. The houses' and condos' bathrooms have been updated.
4. The helicopters' and airplanes' engines have been replaced.
5. Billy's and Willy's cell phones were dropped on the ground.
6. The operators and mechanics' contract is new.
7. The employees and visitors' lounge is large.
8. The boys and girls' audition is today.
9. The first-graders' and second-graders' bikes were locked up.

Warm-Up 129 (page 136)
1. singular
2. plural
3. singular
4. singular
5. plural
6. plural
7. plural
8. plural
9. singular
10. plural

Rewrites:
1. Luis's wallet
2. the bass's bones

Warm-Up 130 (page 137)
1. let's
2. they're
3. you're
4. couldn't
5. they'll
6. I've
7. we'll
8. he's
9. won't
10. wouldn't
11. mustn't
12. didn't
13. isn't
14. can't
15. she'd
16. you'd

Underline the following:
I am
You will
I have
who has
did not
You are
did not
You will
She is
I am
she will
He is
He will
you are
you have

Contractions:
1. I'm
2. You'll
3. I've
4. who's
5. didn't
6. You're
7. didn't
8. You'll
9. She's
10. I'm
11. she'll
12. He's
13. He'll
14. you're
15. you've

Warm-Up 131 (page 138)
1. you would
2. might have
3. they would or they had
4. had not
5. we have
6. they have
7. she will
8. were not
9. do not
10. should not
11. will not
12. we had or we would
13. who is or who has
14. must not
15. has not
16. he will
17. I am
18. they will

1. could not/couldn't
2. will not/won't
3. Who is/Who's
4. Do not/Don't
5. I will/I'll
6. had not/hadn't
7. does not/doesn't
8. They are/They're

Warm-Up 132 (page 139)
1. ice-cream
2. twenty-three
3. well-known
4. high-wire
5. toll-free
6. thirty-nine

Check passage for underlined words needing hyphens.
1. world-renowned
2. ninety-nine
3. rut-filled
4. super-secret
5. wind-weathered
6. Great-Grandma

Warm-Up 133 (page 140)
1. mid-century
2. T-shirts
3. ex-football
4. mayor-elect
5. self-absorbed
6. ex-drummer
7. T-ball
1. cal-ci-fy
2. bul-le-tin
3. sap-ling
4. ther-mom-e-ter
5. crys-tal-lize
6. sub-se-quent
7. un-touch-a-ble
8. whirl-pool
9. e-mol-li-ent
10. cro-quet

Warm-Up 134 (page 141)
Place a colon after: 1, 2, 4, 8.
Place a comma after: 3, 5, 6, 7, 9, 10.
Check the two personal and two formal greetings.

Warm-Up 135 (page 142)
Underline and correct the following greetings:
1. Dear Sir or Madam:
5. To Whom It May Concern:
6. Dear President Thomas:
7. Customer Service:
10. Dear Principal Smith:
1. Surf Like a Pro: Ten Easy Steps to Mastering the Basics
2. The Electoral College: So Confusing Nobody Can Explain It
3. What's Up With That?: 15 Mysteries Easily Explained
4. Iggy: The Man Behind the Name

5. Woolly Mammoth and Man: Did They Ever Walk the Earth Together?
6. Carbonation: The Real Pop Behind Soda Pop
7. Using Your Digital Camera: How to Take Pictures Like a Pro
8. Bottled Water versus Tap Water: The Real Truth
9. Hybrids: Two Kinds of Cars Rolled Into One
10. Cats: Feline or Fiendish?

Warm-Up 136 (page 143)
Check that each sentence was rewritten correctly with a colon.

Warm-Up 137 (page 144)
1. The job requires the following attributes: good speaking skills, great people skills, and hard work.
2. Pack the following items: hiking boots, shorts, sunscreen, and a hat.
3. Michelle read a book, wrote a story, and painted a picture.
4. This is what happened: the boys hit a ball, the ball broke the window, the homeowner was not happy.
5. Roscoe ate the pizza, cookies, hot dogs, and potato chips.
6. In case of an emergency, follow the following steps: get to a safe place, call 9-1-1, stay calm.
7. Tanya reported that the recycling drive raised one hundred dollars and the coat drive provided fifty coats.

Warm-Up 138 (page 145)
1. "Down!" said Dad to the dog.
2. "Marla," said Mrs. Harrison, "Do you need help?"
3. "Go to school!" said Dad.
7. The classmates yelled, "Happy Birthday!"
9. "Have you ever read, *Why Did the Chicken Cross the Road?*" asked the professor.

10. "Shhh, the baby is sleeping," whispered Grandma.
11. Scott yelled, "Yeah Chargers!" when his team scored some points.
13. The principal said, "Good job, the campus looks very clean."
14. The coach asked, "Are there any questions?"
15. "Who made all of these beautiful cards?" asked the principal.

Cross out sentences 4, 5, 6, 8, and 12.

Warm-Up 139 (page 146)
"Guess what!" yelled Mavis.
"What?" asked Dewey.
"I finally made it onto the Principal's List!"
"Wow! That's great, Mavis!"
"Thanks, Dewey. I worked so hard this quarter. I can't believe I made straight A's in all my classes. You know how hard spelling is for me. But I studied hard for every week's spelling test."
"Good for you, Mavis. I made Honor Roll. I had all As and Bs."
"That's great, Dewey! You did a good job, too!" said Mavis.
"Let's go and get a root beer to celebrate!" suggested Dewey.
"Thanks, Dewey. You're a great friend! Let's go get that root beer," said Mavis.

Warm-Up 140 (page 147)
Answers will vary for 1–8.

Tonight is the final episode of "Can They Spell It!" I have been waiting to see this finale for weeks. I can't wait to see if Cash or Chase wins in the showdown. They are both very good. After the show, I will turn on my radio and listen to the recap on "What Happened After the Show?" This program, hosted by R U Listening, has interviews with the contestants and gives a sneak peek as to what happened

behind the scenes. Then, next week, I will read even more about the show in a column called "Spell Watch" in the weekly TV Guide issue. In my current affairs class, I even wrote an essay, "Cash and Chase: the Showdown." My teacher guessed I loved the show!

Warm-Up 141 (page 148)
Check to make sure the student added proper punctuation on the lines and the proofer marks for a paragraph.

Warm-Up 142 (page 149)
Check to make sure the student wrote appropriate titles.

Warm-Up 143 (page 150)
Check the margins for the book. Check to make sure the student indented and rewrote the rest of the paragraph within the margins.

Warm-Up 144 (page 151)
Check that students have used proofer marks correctly.

1. bob and sue like to eat at Ho ming's Restaurant.
2. where is Benicia?
3. The new television season is starting soon.
4. Where Barbara?
5. R the glasses in the dishwasher clean or dirty?
6. the ribbons are for the birthday presents.
7. Mom bought four new tires for in bloom the antique vehicle.
8. A ruler is helpful when measuring small items.
9. The map shows the different routes we can take to get to seattle washington.
10. Mrs. tomlinson taught me to make delicious homemade bread pies and a cake!

Warm-Up 145 (page 152)

1. we like taking our dogs to the local dog park⊙
2. horatio bought a ~~knew~~ [sp new] brand of peanut butter⊙
3. what do you think of the name franklin for my new turtle?
4. how many grains of ~~sea~~ [sp sand] are one teaspoon? [in ∧]
5. Frank and mike give people parking tickets⊙

did you ~~no~~ [sp know] that you can buy ~~nsuenc~~ [sp insurance] for your pet? That's right! Since pets ~~aer~~ [sp are] living longer and being treated mor like family members than animals, many companies are now offering insurance to help your pet live a long and full life⊙ Depending upon the breed of your pet, the ~~kost~~ [sp cost] of the insurance can be cheap or expensive. Before you jump on the insurance bandwagon, check into the costs and see if it would benefit your pet and your budget.

Warm-Up 146 (page 153)
Check that students have used proofer marks correctly.

Parking meters
~~Whenevr~~ [sp Whenever] a driver travels to a big city, the driver might see parking meters. The city ~~place~~ [sp places] parking meters on city streets to generate revenue. ~~hen~~ [sp When] a driver parks ~~on~~ by a parking meter, the driver places coins in the parking meter⊙ The parking meter gives a certain amount of time∧based upon the amount of money fed into the parking meter. Once the time is ~~upp~~ [sp up], the driver needs to move the car or risk getting a parking ticket.

Dog Rescue
Have you ever thought you ~~kould~~ [sp could] save a dog's life? You ~~kan~~ [sp can]! Instead of buying a puppy, why not visit a local animal shelter? At the animal shelter∧you will see all kinds of dogs—big ones, little ones, furry ones, funny ones—a dog to fit any kind ~~ov~~ [sp of] family or lifestyle. by adopting a dog from a shelter, you are not only saving the dog's life∧you are also getting a new best friend.

Warm-Up 147 (page 154)
Check that students have used proofer marks correctly.

Every wednesday night∧our troop hosts bowling night∧the local bowling alley. [at] kids from all over the city can bowl for free∞if they bring a can of soup or a gently used toy to donate to a needy child⊙ The kids are put into teams by ability∧not by age, and then the games begin. For the beginning bowlers, there is bumper bowling. In bumper bowling, inner tubes are put in the gutters. This makes it easier for the beginner bowler to roll the bowling ball down the middle of the lane and not throw "gutter balls⊙" for the intermediate and advanced bowlers, regular lanes ~~aer~~ [sp are] used. After everyone has bowled ~~to~~ [sp two] games, snacks are provided by the bowling alley. All of the bowlers get a hot dog, chips, and a soda. To earn extra money, the troops sell homemade desserts like brownies and cookies. The bowlers get to sit around and visit and make new friends while they eat. It's a great way to learn a sport, meet ~~knew~~ [sp new] people, and help the community out at the same time!

Warm-Up 148 (page 155)

List 1	List 2
alien	blender
astronaut	convection
food	dishwasher
identification	faucet
mechanical	microwave
pack	oven
repair	refrigerator
space	sink
stars	stove
travel	toaster

Warm-Up 149 (page 156)

2. bed-belonging
3. breakfast-cement
4. drain-family
5. fence-frock
6. lattice-mainstream
7. morning-pillow
8. premiere-rested
9. settling-slanted
10. slept-sofa
11. stove-tea
12. web-window

Guide words will vary for 1–6.

Warm-Up 150 (page 157)
Chart will vary depending on dictionary used.

Warm-Up 151 (page 158)
Possible definitions:

1. a type of warfare
2. regard for self or others
3. new or unique
4. length of decorative drapery hung on top of a window
5. drinkable
6. a challenge
7. to wrestle, to round up
8. person who is fanatical
9. become less intense
10. Trademark for a type of photocopy or machine
11. loud and aggressive
12. clumsy
13. movie
14. a type of stitch used by medical professionals
15. trickery

Warm-Up 152 (page 159)

1. n. a traffic light
   v. a gesture or sign to convey information
2. n. place or angle where two sides meet
   v. force into a situation that is difficult to get out of
3. n. location or stop, as in for a train or bus

v. put or assign a specific location
4. n. a curse
   v. to name the letters in a word
1. noun
2. verb
3. verb
4. verb
5. noun
6. noun
7. noun
8. verb

Warm-Up 153 (page 160)
Check that bibliographic information for two books is entered correctly and the question has been answered.

Warm-Up 154 (page 161)

1. 000 or 400
2. 500
3. 900
4. 000
5. 500 or 600
6. 900
7. 700
8. 700
9. 200
10. 900
11. 000
12. 700
13. 700
14. 300

Check the answers to the questions.

Warm-Up 155 (page 162)

1. 580
2. 560
3. 640
4. 690
5. 520
6. 530
7. 550
8. 540
9. 660
10. 610
11. 590
12. 630
13. 660
14. 510
15. 670
16. 650
17. 540
18. 520
19. 640
20. 610

Check the answer to the question.

Warm-Up 156 (page 163)
Check both cards.

Warm-Up 157 (page 164)

1. Cowboys
2. 1998
3. 24
4. Bullock, Ivan
5. I Wish I Were a Cowboy
6. JUN 636.2BUL
7. World Book Publication in association with Two Can, 1998
8. Junior